FLAVORS
OF THE
MAGHREB
& SOUTHERN ITALY

RECIPES FROM
THE LAND OF THE SETTING SUN

FLAVORS
OF THE
MAGHREB
& SOUTHERN ITALY

RECIPES FROM
THE LAND OF THE SETTING SUN

Alba Carbonaro Johnson
Paula Miller Jacobson
Sheilah Kaufman

HIPPOCRENE BOOKS
NEW YORK

Photographs by Alba Carbonaro Johnson and Sandy Ireland except as noted below.

Photos on pages 23, 41, 51, 63, 78, 83, 106, 110-11, 117, and 132 by Maureen Cogan.

Images in Fresh Herbs Guide pages 191-193: "Herbs in pots stock photo" @istockphoto.com/marilyna, "Various bunches of fresh edible greens isolated stock photo" @istockphoto.com/VvoeVale, and "Herbs in Pots with Leaf Sprigs stock photo" @istockphoto.com/marilyna

Images in Spices Guide pages 194-195: "Large set of spices isolated on white" @istockphoto.com/ Dmitrich

Book and cover design by Acme Klong Design

For more information, address:

HIPPOCRENE BOOKS, INC.

171 Madison Avenue

New York, NY 10016

www.hippocrenebooks.com

ISBN 978-0-7818-1436-2

Cataloging-in-publication data available from the Library of Congress.

Printed in the United States of America.

CONTENTS

ABOUT CHEF ALBA

"Ho mangiato alla tavola di miliardari, ed ho mangiato malissimo.
Ho mangiato alla di contadini ed ho mangiato benissimo.
La bontà dei cibi sta nella semplicità e nella genuinità dei prodotti."

"I have eaten at the table of billionaires, and I ate very badly.
I have eaten at the table of farmers, and I ate very well.
The quality of the food is in the simplicity and genuineness of products"
　—source unknown

I was born in Naples, Italy, and raised in Tunis, Tunisia, which was a French colony at the time. I had the luxury of experiencing multicultural cuisines from an early age. As a cooking instructor, cookbook author, and personal chef, I create recipes that are easily identifiable as Maghrebi and I focus on affordable, high-quality, fresh ingredients and ease of preparation. Some of my cooking techniques have been handed down by family members and can be used over and over again in many variations. My dishes are simple, not hidden under fancy sauces or elaborate presentations. My love for cooking and desire to share my culture have always been my passions, which is why I have chosen recipes suitable for cooks of any level of experience. These dishes are what I remember vividly throughout my life and are what inspire me.

Three generations ago, my ancestors emigrated from Sicily to Tunisia, one of the countries in the Maghreb on the Mediterranean Sea. When I was growing up in Tunisia, I learned four languages: French, which was the primary language spoken and taught in schools; Arabic, which was a required second language; Italian, our language of origin, which was spoken at home among family members and friends; and Tunisian, which was a mélange of bits of Italian, French, Arabic, and Sicilian.

The Maghrebi cuisine is well-known for its use of fresh, local, in-season ingredients. This rustic

Maghreb-style cooking is the result of the influence of long-time relationships between the locals and the many foreigners who colonized the region over the centuries. Because of these influences, our gastronomy evolved to become a vibrant, colorful, and spicy national cuisine. The countries of the Maghreb are somewhat similar in climate, landforms, gastronomy, and history, yet each country has its own unique culinary customs and traditions.

Maghrebi cuisine is varied and enriched through its use of fresh herbs and spices. One of the most popular dishes in the Maghreb is couscous, which is made by steaming semolina. *Seffa* Couscous—made with dried fruits, nuts, brown sugar, and cinnamon—is served at weddings, celebrations of birth, and other festive occasions. In my family, we ate couscous often, except on Sundays. On Sundays, for our special main dish we would prepare a pasta sauce that cooked for several hours. Sunday was the day when the entire family would gather in one home and share and delight in diverse dishes with our friends. Our Sunday meals concluded with sweets made with simple syrup; abundant seasonal fruits, such as dates, figs, oranges, mandarins, watermelons, and grapes; and nuts such as almonds and hazelnuts.

Sharing a meal with others is an honored tradition and an expression of hospitality and generosity. This tradition we honored in our Italian homes as well. I learned early on as a small child that it is important to make sure that a variety of food options are served at the table to please our guests. I was taught to taste dishes many times while cooking to make sure that they are well seasoned. Preparing a variety of memorable and inviting appetizers, salads, entrées, and vegetables was a gracious way to demonstrate to our guests that they were most welcome in our home.

Let me tell you how I developed a passion for Maghrebi cuisine. My grandfather had just retired from working as a marble mason. He had an incredible sense of humor and a passion for cooking. My grandfather convinced my grandmother that she deserved time off from the kitchen after all the years of cooking and raising six children. However, I think it was his brilliant plan to show off his cooking skills, which he thought were superior to hers, but, of course, he would never tell her that. So, there began my cooking adventures with my grandfather.

Since we lived practically next door to my grandparents, my grandfather would come to get me every day, and we would walk together to the open market to purchase fresh ingredients for the day's meals. He didn't call out my name; he whistled a tune that was specifically meant for me to hear and to understand that he was waiting to take me to the market. I learned through observation how to be selective in choosing the freshest fish, vegetables, and fruits, as well as how to bargain over their prices. Every day was an exciting new adventure for me, and I looked forward to open-market outings with my grandfather. Each day, all the way to the market, he would describe what he intended to cook in the hope that all of the ingredients would be available and as fresh as possible. As he made his selections, he would explain to me in the presence of the merchants how to know when a fruit or vegetable was at its freshest.

In our tiny kitchens, most of us had only a small two-burner stove, no ovens, and either a very small refrigerator or no refrigerator at all. So, the shopping and cooking had to be planned daily because there was no place to store fresh food. It was very common for people to prepare their own bread from scratch daily then take it to the nearest bakery to have it baked for a small fee. Most of the time, it was the children who were sent to the baker to deliver the bread dough and to pick up the baked bread. I still remember going to the bakery and the aroma of freshly baked bread that filled my nose from a few blocks away. While waiting in line to pick up the bread, I'd close my eyes and visualize loaves dancing out of the oven and one of them landing right under my nose. The hardest thing for me was to resist the temptation of pulling off a piece before I got it home to my parents. Let's just say that I didn't always succeed.

Because the climate was usually bright, sunny, and warm, we cooked outdoors most of the time. My grandfather had concocted a little outdoor stove, somewhat prehistoric but functional. There was no air conditioning inside, so cooking outside was cooler because we lived near a port and there was always a cool breeze. As I got a little older, my grandfather began to allow me to cook. Step by step, he would instruct me from the moment we selected and bargained for our fresh ingredients at the open market until we prepared the meal. I learned to scale fish, cut meats, and chop vegetables, all by the time I was eight years old. He taught me how to use all of my senses as tools to become a better cook. At the market, he would show me how to smell to know when fish was fresh. We used sight and touch to check if a vegetable or fruit was ripe enough or too ripe. He reminded me how important the sense of taste is when checking for proper seasoning several times during the cooking process. Even hearing is important during the cooking process: the sizzling of an onion going into hot oil, the bubbling of simmering sauce, and the slap of dough being kneaded.

You could say that I learned from a masterful mind the art of planning and creating meals, knowing how to select the freshest ingredients, learning how to bargain for value, and using my senses to create delicious food. Perhaps some of this can be learned at a culinary school; the adventure that goes with it, however, cannot.

I always reminisce over the wonderful times I had with my grandfather—each day a new adventure. I looked forward to the proud look on his face when the family took the first bites of his delicious dishes and he saw the delighted expressions on their faces as they enjoyed his well-prepared and extraordinary food. These are the memories of my grandfather that I will always deeply treasure. These are recollections that I want to share with you, my readers and the students who attend my cooking classes. I look forward to your facial expressions when you take your first bites during my cooking classes.

There are many special people in my life who have inspired me. Perhaps someone has inspired you, too, and made you want to learn more ways to express your inner soul by cooking traditional dishes for your family and friends. Or, it may be an inborn curiosity or love of food that gives you the passion to want to learn more. To learn more, we read cookbooks, watch food programs, attend cooking classes, and cook with friends and family.

When you begin to cook my recipes, remember to practice cooking intuitively and creatively with whatever ingredients are at hand. When you go to the market, buy what's available in season, and what looks and smells good enough to cook that day. If you cannot find the vegetable you are looking for, substitute another vegetable you like. Modify the recipe to suit your own taste. Think of my ingredients and the directions on my recipes as a guide. Once you have made my recipes a few times, you can create your own versions, and evolve to creating your own traditions for your family.

WHAT IS THE MEDITERRANEAN TO ME?

The Mediterranean region is a veranda that overlooks the azure sea and the horizon and allows me to enjoy the warmth of the sun and the colors and perfumes of luxuriant vegetation. This warm, inviting atmosphere puts me at ease and makes me want to enjoy it in the company of friends. I gain appreciation for the region's quality ingredients and products. I share in the pleasure and the understanding that eating food is about the gathering of family and friends at the table for enjoyment, conversation, tradition, and continuing the culture.

The climate, together with the soil, is one of the main elements that defines the types of crops that grow in the Mediterranean region. The Mediterranean climate is distinguished by erratic rainfall and mild temperatures. Irregular landscapes and diverse soil types in the areas encircling the Mediterranean Sea allow for a wide variety of crops and plants. In these areas, the climate is tempered by the presence of this sea. An abundance of plants is native to this area; some flourish only in this area. Plants typical of the Mediterranean are appreciated for their beauty and the edible ones for their taste.

Citrus fruits—lemons, oranges, and grapefruits—grow well in the Mediterranean region because citrus trees have a similar root structure to olive trees. The thick skins of citrus fruits are well-adapted to the Mediterranean climate.

An essential oil produced from myrtle leaves is used not only in perfumes but also in medicines for its disinfectant benefits. Myrtle's bluish-black berries ripen on the plant in late summer. In Italy, especially on the Island of Sardinia, these berries are used to make an excellent liqueur called *Liquore di Mirto*.

The olive tree is of major agricultural importance in the Mediterranean region. The fruit of the tree is used both for consumption and in the production of olive oil. Olive trees, like fig and date trees, have widespread roots and limited foliage, which allow them to adapt well to the climate and soil quality in much of the Mediterranean basin.

The Maghreb does not have many grazing animals. Plants with shallow roots, like grass, do not grow well. Without grass, grazing animals like cows and sheep do not have food to eat, and grain-fed cow farming is not a common practice. As a result, people cook with olive oil instead of with animal fat.

Grapes, cultivated both for eating and for making wine, grow very well thanks to the mild temperatures and ideal moisture conditions in many areas. Each subregion has grapes that offer specific flavors: Palomino grapes for sherry are grown in the Andalusia region of Spain, Nero d'Avola grapes in Sicily, and Patrimonio region grapes in Corsica.

In most of the Mediterranean countries, the majority of cultivated crops are fresh vegetables, including eggplant, tomatoes, broccoli, cabbage, zucchini, cucumber, and pulses. Pulses—beans, peas, chickpeas, and lentils—are the edible seeds of plants in the legume family. Some plants, such as

rosemary and capers, grow spontaneously. Rosemary is found growing throughout the coasts of the Mediterranean. Its natural habitat is in the steep rocks and cliffs, from the sunny inland to the maritime coasts. The rosemary plant can reach a height of ten feet. It even grows well in poor soil and limestone. The caper plant thrives in very stony areas as well and can reach a height of twenty feet.

The Mediterranean diet, which is recognized on UNESCO's list of the Intangible Cultural Heritage of Humanity, is an eating lifestyle based on centuries of traditional foods inspired by countries nestled around the Mediterranean Sea: Italy, Spain, France, Greece, Turkey, Morocco, Tunisia, and Algeria. The diet favors cereals, fruits, vegetables, seeds, and olive oil (unsaturated fat), with moderate consumption of fish, white meat, legumes, eggs, dairy products, red wine, and sweets, and minimal consumption of red meat and animal fats (saturated fats).

Let's take a culinary tour of a luxurious cuisine from the warm and fascinating lands of the Maghreb, a region of the Mediterranean. Maghrebi cuisine is a reflection of the environment that is deeply rooted in the people of this Mediterranean world. It invokes the senses of smell and sight; it tastes like no other cuisine. The magic behind Maghrebi cuisine is in its ingredients: vivid vegetables and fruits, exotic spices, aromatic warm bread, and saffron, sweet rosewater, and fresh mint with their voluptuous scents. These sensuous qualities make up the essence of Mediterranean food.

—Alba Carbonaro Johnson

THE EXOTIC MAGHREB

The word "Maghreb" means "Land of the Setting Sun." The Maghreb is a multicultural Mediterranean region of North Africa which includes Tunisia, Algeria, Morocco, Mauritania, and Libya. It is bordered by the beautiful Mediterranean Sea. In ancient times, the Maghreb included parts of Spain, Sicily, and Malta. The history of this region is different from that of the rest of Africa, and today's cuisine reflects those differences.

Before the Arab conquest, the Phoenicians, Greeks, Romans, Byzantines, and later the Italians and French, colonized the Maghreb. These civilizations contributed heavily to the ethnic composition of its people and the development of its culture and cuisine. Each new culture that entered the region left unique influences, and together they created a colorful, multicultural cuisine using aromatic spices, fresh herbs, citrus, dried fruits, nuts, fresh fish, lamb, chicken, pasta, rice, and lots of fresh vegetables. Ancient civilizations such as Phoenicians and Romans spread the cultivation of wheat. The Moors brought citrus and olives from Spain. The Berbers gave birth to couscous. Fennel, peas, and artichokes arrived with the Italian settlement, and the baguette, salad Niçoise, and mayonnaise were brought by the French when they colonized the area. Thus, the food of the Maghreb became a mélange of Sicilian, French, Spanish, Arabic, and Berber cuisine. It's an inviting cuisine, made with fresh local and seasonal ingredients, that carries a diversity of flavors and time-honored traditions to the Maghreb table.

The countries of the Maghreb have a common style of cooking using tasty spices and dried fruits in meat dishes. Cinnamon, cumin, coriander, ginger, turmeric, paprika, figs, apricots, prunes, and golden raisins all combine to enhance other ingredients in the food. Couscous is the national dish of the Maghreb. It can be made with the catch of the day, lamb, stuffed vegetables, or golden raisins and is served with spicy harissa. Salads and prepared vegetables are always served in abundance as an accompaniment to the main dishes. Desserts consist of fresh oranges, mandarins, and melons to cool the palate. Sweet pastries are made with almonds or pistachios and are served with a simple syrup or honey.

In the Maghreb, cooking is more than simply preparing food to satisfy one's hunger; it is an expression of love in creating a carefully and beautifully prepared repast. Dinner guests can anticipate enjoying an abundance of memorable inviting dishes that were prepared especially for them. Serving a special meal is a way to communicate that guests are most welcome and to encourage them to return.

Bring the simple techniques and exotic aromas, colors, and flavors of the Maghreb to life and create your own traditions when you make these recipes.

WHY IT'S BETTER TO EAT PRODUCE IN SEASON

Today, with the arrival of modern greenhouses and new shipping means, nearly all fruits and vegetables can be eaten year-round. Yet, the taste of fresh vegetables and fruits that have been refrigerated in compartments for weeks or even months cannot compare to the ones harvested locally or shipped immediately while in season. By being exposed to natural light, rather than artificial cold, local fresh vegetables retain their antioxidants that come from the sun and then bring their many benefits to our entire bodies. Changing the foods on our table according to the seasons also means diversifying the intake of vitamins, minerals, and other nutrients that our bodies need. And, if we choose organic produce, we can feel confident that we are not ingesting pesticides, fertilizers, and other harmful and artificial agents.

If we want to experience the heart and soul of what makes food divine, we have to eat what's in season. This is a value that is deeply ingrained in me. Maghrebi cooking is a sustainable regimen that respects the environment and its cultural traditions. The secret lies in local, and, most importantly, seasonal ingredients. By eating seasonal produce, you're eating fresh ingredients at the height of their flavor. You will not want to go back to jarred food or deep-frozen ingredients that may have been preserved for months or years. If you eat ingredients in the optimal months, you will experience the very best of a cuisine. What better way to experience one of the world's greatest cuisines than to approach it with the care and respect that it deserves?

Here are important reasons to buy and eat fruits and vegetables in season:

Taste and Aroma: Fresh produce that is harvested according to its natural maturation is a remarkable delicacy for our palates. Freshly ripened fruits and vegetables have an unparalleled flavor, have their own characteristic aroma, and are much more colorful than hothouse foods. Out-of-season produce leaves a lot to be desired in quality and taste; it is preferable to follow the natural cycle of fruits and vegetables.

Environmental Choice: The growing of fruits and vegetables out of season increases the pollution on our planet, so it's important to consume fruits and vegetables that are environmentally friendly. The industrial process necessary to grow those out-of-season fruits and vegetables involves the use of artificial energy, often coming from fossil fuels, to heat and keep greenhouses lighted. In addition, because produce grown out of season is grown outside of its natural habitats, it needs to be transported—those transports produce pollution.

Nutrition: Seasonal fruits and vegetables are more nutritious because they follow their natural cycles, making them richer in essential nutrients that are necessary for the well-being of our bodies. Fruits and vegetables need to ripen on their vines or trees, as nature intended, to boost the amounts of vitamins and minerals.

Reduction of pesticides: Products grown seasonally and organically will have much lower quantities of pesticides. The vegetables and fruits that are forced to grow against their natural cycle are weaker and therefore are more vulnerable to insects, requiring an increased use of pesticides.

Lower Price: Nonseasonal fruits and vegetables cost more in order to cover the increased costs of being imported and transported over long distances.

APPETIZERS

COLD

Roasted Garlic, Capers, and Sesame Dipping Oil
Chickpeas with Lemon and Parmesan
Chunky Spicy Hummus
Crostini with Dill and Pecorino
Crostini with Ricotta and Orange Zest
Marinated Steamed Mussels

HOT

Fennel Frittelle
Baked Olives in a Crust
Cauliflower Frittelle
Grilled Bell Pepper, Onion, and Tomato Salad
Potato and Egg Croquettes
Red Onion and Mint Frittelle

Appetizers are small portions of savory foods
that are served before the main meal. A first course
is meant to stimulate or whet the appetite while guests
wait for the main dishes to be served. Maghrebi countries
serve several small plates not only to stimulate the appetite
but also to prolong family time and conversations. Appetizers
can be either cold or hot and are always served with warm bread.
In the Maghreb, appetizers are made with simple, fresh, and colorful
quality ingredients and are enhanced by a wise use of spices—a real
delight for the eyes and the palate.

ROASTED GARLIC, CAPERS, AND SESAME DIPPING OIL

Makes 2 cups

This dish is very fragrant. I serve it with crusty bread, in mashed potatoes or mashed cauliflower, and on top of steaks, pork chops, fish, or shellfish. It also is a flavorful pasta sauce: I toss the pasta and the dipping oil together, and then add some fresh chopped basil on top.

25 to 30 cloves garlic, peeled and left whole
1 ½ cups extra virgin olive oil
1 teaspoon red pepper flakes
1 teaspoon dried thyme leaves
1 teaspoon dried oregano leaves
20 to 25 capers in brine, drained
2 tablespoons sesame seeds
Kosher salt
Freshly ground black pepper
2 to 3 tablespoons grated Parmesan
Warm bread for serving

Place the garlic and oil in a deep medium skillet. Cook over low heat, stirring occasionally, 5 to 8 minutes. Add red pepper flakes, thyme, oregano, capers, and sesame seeds. Season with salt and pepper. Cook until the garlic has turned golden. Cool slightly.

Spoon a few tablespoons of the garlic mixture into small serving dishes. Sprinkle Parmesan on top and serve with warm bread.

CHICKPEAS WITH LEMON AND PARMESAN
Serves 4 to 6

Chickpeas have been well-known since ancient Egypt where they were considered food for the poor and slaves. The ancient Romans appreciated the chickpeas and served them fried in olive oil. Chickpeas are a staple in Maghrebi cuisine because of their versatility—they can be boiled, baked, and fried. They can also be used to make hummus, and in soups, pasta dishes, salads, and many side dishes. Chickpeas with Lemon and Parmesan can be served as a cold appetizer or a side dish.

Note: *If you use a microplane to grate the Parmesan extra fine, it will melt right into the dish very quickly.*

1 (28-ounce) can chickpeas, drained well
2 to 3 tablespoons extra virgin olive oil
2 to 3 cloves garlic, minced
1 pinch red pepper flakes
Zest and juice of 1 lemon, divided
1 cup extra-finely grated Parmesan
⅓ cup roughly chopped fresh Italian parsley leaves

Place the chickpeas in a heatproof bowl.

In a small skillet, heat the oil over medium-low heat. Add the garlic, red pepper flakes, and lemon zest, and sauté for about 90 seconds. Transfer the mixture to the bowl with the chickpeas. Immediately add the lemon juice, Parmesan, and parsley. Toss to combine. Serve at room temperature.

CHUNKY SPICY HUMMUS

Makes 3 cups

Chickpeas are the seeds of a plant *(cicer arietinum)* native to the Middle East. The chickpea plant is one of the most popular in the Mediterranean. Hummus is a classic dish in Maghrebi cuisine and is usually served with pita bread and olives. It can also be used as an alternative to mayonnaise for sandwiches. I keep several cans of chickpeas in my pantry for when I get the urge to make a quick hummus appetizer.

1 (28-ounce) can chickpeas, drained, reserve 1 tablespoon chickpeas for garnish
4 to 6 cloves garlic, roughly chopped
1 teaspoon ground cumin
1 teaspoon ground coriander
1 cup tahini
Zest and juice of 1 lemon
¼ cup extra virgin olive oil, plus more for drizzling
¼ to ½ teaspoon Harissa (page 188)
½ cup warm water, if needed
Kosher salt
Freshly ground black pepper
1 tablespoon chopped fresh Italian parsley leaves, for garnish
Toasted pita bread or vegetables for serving

In a food processor, combine the chickpeas, garlic, cumin, coriander, tahini, lemon zest and juice, olive oil, and Harissa. Pulse until the mixture is just slightly chunky. If it is too thick, add a little warm water, a few tablespoons at a time, to get it to the consistency you like. Add salt and pepper a little at a time, tasting after each addition.

Spoon the mixture onto a serving dish and spread flat. Run a fork in a circle around the hummus to create a design. Drizzle a few drops of olive oil on top. Scatter reserved 1 tablespoon whole chickpeas and the parsley on top. Serve with toasted pita bread or vegetables.

Tip: *For additional flavor, sprinkle some ground cumin, coriander, paprika, or even some lemon zest on top of the hummus before serving. Or make a well in the center and fill it with a variety of chopped olives.*

CROSTINI WITH DILL AND PECORINO
Serves 4 to 6

Crostini means "little crusts" in Italian. It is an appetizer made with slices of bread that are toasted until golden and then topped with a variety of savory or sweet toppings. Dill is an herb that is very much like the green feathery leaves of a fennel. Dill is not just for pickling; in the Maghreb, it is popular in pasta dishes, soup, salads, fish, and vegetables. I love the fresh fragrance of dill. The combination of the sweetness of dill with the sharpness of pecorino is perfect with the crunch of the crostini.

12 (½-inch) slices French bread
2 cups roughly chopped fresh dill
6 ounces freshly grated pecorino
4 cloves garlic, sliced paper thin
2 tablespoons extra virgin olive oil
1 pinch red pepper flakes
2 plum tomatoes, finely diced (optional)

Toast the bread slices briefly on the grill or in the oven at 400°F, just until golden on one side.

Place the dill and pecorino in a bowl. Mix in the garlic, oil, and red pepper flakes. Distribute evenly onto the tops of the crostini slices. Return to the oven and bake until the pecorino starts to melt slightly. Transfer to a serving plate, and top with the tomatoes, if using. Serve cold or at room temperature.

CROSTINI WITH RICOTTA AND ORANGE ZEST

Serves 4 to 6

Making crostini is a clever way to use up day-old bread. I came up with this combination because I love fresh ricotta and orange zest, just like we use in cannoli. I wanted to create a savory dish with these ingredients, so I decided to use them to top a crostini. If you prefer lemon zest, by all means try it instead of the orange.

12 (½-inch) slices French bread
2 cloves garlic, peeled and left whole
6 ounces fresh whole milk ricotta
Kosher salt
Freshly ground black pepper
Strips of zest of 1 large orange
Extra virgin olive oil for drizzling

Heat the oven to 400°F.

Lay the slices of bread in one layer on a baking sheet. Place on the middle rack of the oven, and bake until tops are just golden, 3 to 4 minutes. When the slices are ready, remove from the oven and immediately rub the fresh garlic on each toasted top.

Place a tablespoon of ricotta on top of each slice. Sprinkle with pinches of salt and pepper to taste, and the orange zest. Top with a drizzle of olive oil.

Tip: *The bread slices can also be toasted on the grill.*

MARINATED
STEAMED MUSSELS
Serves 4 to 6

If you love mussels, you'll have to try this mussel salad. It's a fresh summer dish, perfect to serve as an appetizer or light seafood dinner. It can be made ahead and served to guests quickly. Whenever I am planning a dinner party, I always make sure that my appetizers are ready to be served, so I can enjoy conversations with my guests when they arrive.

When I was a child, mussels were readily available at a very cheap price. At least once a week, my grandfather would take me to the port to help him pick out a few dozen fresh mussels to prepare for an appetizer or a pasta dish for that day.

1 pound mussels, cleaned and debearded
2 tablespoons extra virgin olive oil
Juice of 1 lemon
3 cloves garlic, minced
1 pinch red pepper flakes
½ bunch fresh Italian parsley leaves, roughly chopped
20 large fresh mint leaves, roughly torn
1 tablespoon capers in brine, drained, roughly chopped
Kosher salt
Freshly ground black pepper
Crusty bread for serving

Check to make sure that all the mussels are closed. Discard any mussels that are open or that have open cracks; they are not edible. Place the mussels in a large skillet over medium-high heat. It is not necessary to add any liquid. Cover and steam until the mussels all open, 5 to 6 minutes. If any mussels are still closed after steaming, discard them; they are not edible. Remove the cooked mussels from the shells and place them in a bowl. Discard the shells.

Meanwhile, place the oil, lemon juice, garlic, red pepper flakes, parsley, mint, and capers in a bowl. Season with salt and pepper; mix well. Transfer the sauce to the bowl with the warm mussels. Toss to combine. Cover and allow to marinate for a few hours in the refrigerator. Serve cold or at room temperature with a nice crusty bread to soak up the juices!

FENNEL FRITTELLE

Serves 6 to 8

Fennel can be eaten raw like celery or can be cooked. Eating raw fennel is refreshing, especially in the summertime. My grandfather used fennel to make cold salads in the summer and *frittelle* whenever his two chickens decided to lay eggs. In Southern Italy, fennel is used in lots of cooked pasta, fish, vegetable, and soup dishes. For me, fennel is a perfect vegetable to use for *frittelle* because it takes on a sweeter and milder flavor when cooked. I serve these *frittelle* as an appetizer, a side dish, or a snack.

2 fennel bulbs
1 cup unbleached all-purpose flour
2 large eggs, beaten
4 tablespoons cold water
2 tablespoons Marsala wine
2 teaspoons fresh thyme leaves
1 pinch kosher salt
Freshly ground black pepper
Extra virgin olive oil for frying
4 to 6 tablespoons grated Parmesan
4 to 6 sprigs fresh Italian parsley leaves

Cut the stems and feathery greens off the fennel bulb and reserve them for soup. Trim and discard a very thin slice from the base. Then slice the bulb in half lengthwise from top to bottom. Cut each half into ¼-inch wide half-moon slices.

Fill a large bowl with ice water. Bring a large saucepan of water to a boil. Add the fennel slices to the boiling water and blanch about 2 minutes. Drain the fennel and immediately plunge it into the ice water. Drain well, and dry with paper towels. Make sure that the fennel slices are completely dry before making the *frittelle*.

Prepare the batter: In a large bowl, mix the flour, eggs, water, wine, thyme, and salt. Season with the pepper. Mix everything together well. Cover and refrigerate to let rest for 1 hour.

Line a baking sheet with paper towels; set aside.

In a large skillet, heat ⅛ inch oil until hot over medium heat. Dip one slice of fennel at a time in the batter, shaking off any excess, and carefully place in the skillet. Cook each *frittella* until golden, 1½ to 2 minutes on each side, turning only once. Do not overcrowd the pan. Continue this process until you have used up all of the ingredients. Place cooked *frittelle* on the prepared paper towels to drain any excess oil. Transfer to a serving dish, and sprinkle with Parmesan and fresh parsley. Serve warm.

BAKED OLIVES IN A CRUST

Serves 4 to 6

Olives are the edible fruit of the olive tree, which is native to the Mediterranean. The main use of olives is the production of olive oil, which has been used since ancient times. Today, olives are used not only for olive oil but also in cocktails, appetizers, and main dishes. In Sicily, olives are put in a small bowl with a drizzle of olive oil but are also paired with other ingredients and baked or fried. Whenever I make these little bundles in my cooking classes, I see surprised and happy expressions on my students' faces.

¾ cup unbleached all-purpose flour
½ cup freshly grated Parmesan
4 tablespoons unsalted butter, at room temperature
½ teaspoon finely minced fresh rosemary leaves
3 tablespoons cold water
20 pitted medium green olives, patted dry
1 large egg

In a bowl, quickly mix the flour, Parmesan, butter, rosemary, and water to combine well. Roll dough into a ¾-inch diameter log; it should be about 15 inches long. Wrap in waxed paper. Chill in the refrigerator for about 2 hours.

Remove the log from the refrigerator. Cut the log into ¾-inch slices. Wrap each slice around one olive, bringing the dough up to enclose the olive. Roll between your palms to form a smooth ball. Place balls on a tray. Cover and refrigerate 1 hour.

Heat oven to 350°F. Line a baking sheet with parchment paper.

Beat the egg with 1½ teaspoons water. Brush each ball all over lightly with the egg wash. Transfer to the prepared baking sheet. Bake for 10 minutes, turn over, and bake until golden, another 5 to 10 minutes. Cool slightly and serve.

CAULIFLOWER FRITTELLE

Serves 6 to 8

Not having a lot of money when I was a child, we needed to be creative with leftovers. Making *frittelle* (fritters) was a delicious way to use leftover vegetables with fresh eggs. *Frittelle* and a slice of bread would certainly fill the belly. This is a dish I make often when I see cauliflower on sale. My kids were not fond of cauliflower, yet whenever I made these *frittelle*, they ate many of them. Cauliflower *Frittelle* is a dish I am proud to serve to family or guests.

1 head cauliflower, cut into florets
Kosher salt
½ cup finely grated carrots
4 to 5 tablespoons unbleached all-purpose flour
3 large eggs, beaten
1½ cups shredded Parmesan, plus more for serving
2 tablespoons minced fresh Italian parsley leaves, plus more for serving
Freshly ground black pepper
Extra virgin olive oil for frying

In a medium saucepan, boil the florets in salted water until completely tender, 5 to 8 minutes. Reserving ½ cup of the water, drain well in a colander. While the cauliflower is still in the colander, press it with your fingertips or a fork to release any remaining water.

In a large bowl, using a fork, mash the cauliflower to a rough but even consistency (or use a food processor and pulse 3 to 4 times). Press out as much liquid as you can. Measure 6 cups of the cauliflower; reserve any remaining cauliflower for another use. Return the cauliflower to the large bowl. Add the carrots, 4 tablespoons flour, and eggs; mix well. Next, add the Parmesan, and parsley. Season with salt and pepper. Combine well. The consistency should be like thick pancake batter. If it's too thin, add a little more flour; if it's too thick, add some reserved water.

Line a baking sheet with paper towels; set aside.

Pour ⅛ inch oil into a large nonstick skillet. Heat the oil over medium-high heat. Scoop ¼ cup portions of the cauliflower mixture and drop them gently into the oil, three or four at a time. Do not overcrowd the pan. Allow each *frittella* to cook undisturbed for a few minutes before turning it over to the other side. The *frittelle* should be golden on top and bottom, 2 to 3 minutes per side. Continue this process until you have used up all of the cauliflower mixture. If the skillet becomes too dry toward the end of the frying process, add a drizzle of oil. If the *frittelle* are browning too quickly, reduce the heat slightly. As the *frittelle* are ready, place them on the prepared paper towels to drain any excess oil. Top these warm *frittelle* with additional parsley and shredded cheese—try to eat just one!

GRILLED BELL PEPPER, ONION, AND TOMATO SALAD

Serves 6 to 8

Mechouia is a typical Tunisian appetizer composed primarily of vegetables such as bell peppers, tomatoes, and onions that are first grilled, then peeled and chopped. It is usually garnished with a drizzle of olive oil, a squeeze of lemon juice, quartered hard-cooked eggs, and sometimes canned albacore tuna. I can't remember a Sunday dinner without *mechouia* at the table. My grandfather's version was made with a few grilled hot spicy peppers, which made it a little spicier than the typical recipe. If you are adventurous, grill one or two hot peppers and add them to your dish.

3 green bell peppers
2 red bell peppers
1 large sweet onion
1 large ripe tomato
3 large cloves garlic, minced
1½ teaspoons ground cumin
1 teaspoon red pepper flakes
⅓ cup extra virgin olive oil, plus more for drizzling

Kosher salt
Freshly ground black pepper
½ lemon
3 to 4 sprigs fresh cilantro or Italian parsley
  leaves, roughly chopped
3 or 4 hard-cooked eggs, quartered
1 (5-ounce) can albacore tuna in olive oil, drained

Heat the grill to medium-high. Place the peppers, onion, and tomato on the grill, and cook, turning occasionally, until most of the surface is charred. The onion may take the longest to cook. When the peppers, onion, and tomato are fully roasted, cool for a few minutes, remove the skins and any seeds. Cut the vegetables into thin slices or small dice. They must all be cut about the same size whether you slice or dice them. *Mechouia* should be chunky.

Place grilled vegetables, garlic, cumin, red pepper flakes, and oil in a large bowl. Season with salt and pepper. Mix well to combine. Taste for seasoning and adjust if needed. Transfer to a serving plate. Squeeze fresh lemon juice over the vegetables. Add fresh chopped herbs, and drizzle with a little olive oil. Garnish with some hard-cooked egg quarters and flaked tuna.

POTATO AND EGG CROQUETTES
Serves 4 to 6

The word "croquette" is derived from the French "*croquer*," which means crunchy. A croquette is a small oval fried patty usually made with leftovers, having mashed potatoes as one of the main ingredients. We made these goodies when we had leftover potatoes and ate them as a snack. When I was a child, I looked forward to getting the eggs from the chickens at my grandparents' home, because I knew something good was going to be cooking that day. I make these croquettes for brunch guests and in my cooking classes; they are a huge hit every time. I also love serving them as a tapas dish with a side of aioli.

2 pounds Yukon Gold potatoes, peeled
Kosher salt
2 tablespoons unsalted butter
1 pinch red pepper flakes
4 tablespoons grated Parmesan
20 fresh basil leaves, torn into tiny pieces
Freshly ground black pepper
10 large hard-cooked eggs, peeled
1 cup unbleached all-purpose flour
2 large eggs, beaten
1 cup dry Italian bread crumbs
Extra virgin olive oil for frying

Place the potatoes in a medium saucepan with enough cold water to cover the potatoes. Bring to a boil over high heat. Reduce heat to medium-low. Add 1 tablespoon salt, partially cover, and simmer until tender, about 10 minutes. Drain well and mash while still hot. Add the butter, red pepper flakes, Parmesan, and basil. Season with salt and pepper. Mix well; set aside to cool.

Divide the potato mixture into 10 equal portions. Make a depression in each portion and place a hard-cooked egg inside. Bring the potato up and around the egg to enclose it completely. Gently roll the croquette between your palms to even out and smooth the potato layer.

Place the flour, beaten eggs, and bread crumbs in three individual shallow bowls. Coat each croquette with the flour first, then the beaten egg, and lastly with the bread crumbs. Be sure to shake off any excess bread crumbs.

Line a baking sheet with paper towels.

Pour ⅛ inch oil into a large nonstick skillet and heat over medium heat. When the oil is hot, fry the croquettes until lightly browned on all sides. Do not overcrowd the skillet. Cook them in batches and place each croquette on the prepared paper towels to absorb any excess oil. Serve warm or at room temperature.

RED ONION AND MINT FRITTELLE

Serves 4 to 6

My mother could make *frittelle* with almost any vegetable. Onions were very inexpensive, and mint grew in every front yard. Because I was a picky eater as a child, she would add extra grated cheese for me.

Onion *frittelle* come alive when the onions are shredded and fried. How smart was the first person to create this savory recipe with such simple ingredients! The mild sweetness of the red onion, combined with the freshness of the mint, makes magnificent *frittelle*.

1 pound red onions
3 to 4 tablespoons finely torn fresh mint leaves, plus more for serving
½ cup grated pecorino, plus more for serving
1 pinch red pepper flakes
Kosher salt
Freshly ground black pepper
2 cups unbleached all-purpose flour
Extra virgin olive oil for frying

With the large side of a grater, shred the onions into a large bowl. Add the mint, pecorino, and red pepper flakes. Season with salt and pepper. Add the flour a little at a time until the mixture becomes a dense batter. You may not need to use all the flour. Mix well. The batter should be the consistency of pancake batter. If the batter is not thick enough, add a little more flour. If it is too thick, simply add a little cold water.

Line a baking sheet with paper towels.

Heat ⅛ inch oil in a large skillet over medium heat. When the oil is hot, pour 1 heaping tablespoon of onion batter at a time into the oil, keeping the *frittelle* separated so they will not stick together. Cook the *frittelle* just like little pancakes until evenly browned on each side, turning only once. Continue this process until you have used up all the batter. Place the cooked *frittelle* on the prepared paper towels to absorb any extra oil. Transfer to a serving dish and serve warm with a little more grated cheese and fresh mint on top.

SOUPS

Chickpea and Swiss Chard Soup
Escarole and Cannellini Bean Soup
Fish and Fennel Soup
Onion, Celery, and Couscous Soup
Pumpkin and Ditalini Soup
Spicy Cauliflower Soup
Velvety Chickpea and Pasta Soup
Bread Soup

When autumn arrives and the temperature drops, I have an irresistible craving for soup. I want to wrap myself up and eat something comforting. With vegetables, legumes, meat or fish, and water or broth, soup is the perfect first course—warming and welcoming on any table. Every Maghrebi and Mediterranean region has its own traditional soup; there is never a shortage of soup recipes. Soup is a product of *cucina povera*, the cooking of the poor, yet it is consistently rich in flavor. A soup is simple to make. Once you have selected the necessary ingredients, you clean and cut them up, and add them to the pot to simmer slowly on the stove. The best soups are made with the best quality ingredients. Soups are probably the most appreciated dishes not only for their simplicity in preparation, but also for their excellent nutritional properties and their wonderful mix of flavors.

CHICKPEA AND SWISS CHARD SOUP

Serves 4 to 6

My mother's favorite vegetable was Swiss chard, so she was very imaginative in finding dishes to use it in. She used it in stews; she sautéed it with tomatoes; she coated it with batter and fried it. There are too many varieties to list them all. Chickpea and Swiss Chard Soup is a dish that even a picky eater like me enjoyed each time my mother made it. This Arabic soup has been adapted by many Italian regions with lots of variations. Add toasted bread, and this healthful and nutritious soup becomes a complete delicious meal.

2 to 3 tablespoons extra virgin olive oil, plus more for drizzling
1 large sweet onion, minced
2 cloves garlic, minced
1 (15-ounce) can plum tomatoes, with juice, diced
1 teaspoon red pepper flakes
1 teaspoon ground cumin
1 teaspoon ground coriander
½ pound Swiss chard, leaves only, chopped
2 cups canned chickpeas, drained
8 cups vegetable broth
Kosher salt
Freshly ground black pepper
4 to 6 slices rustic bread, toasted
½ lemon

Heat the oil in a large saucepan over medium heat. Add the onions and sauté until translucent, 5 to 6 minutes. Add the garlic, and sauté for another minute. Stir in the tomatoes and their juice

and cook for 5 to 8 minutes. Add the red pepper flakes, cumin, coriander, and Swiss chard; sauté 2 minutes. Add the chickpeas and broth and bring to a boil. Taste for seasoning and add salt and pepper, if needed.

Reduce heat to low, and simmer, covered, until vegetables are fully cooked, 5 to 10 minutes. Place 1 slice of toasted bread on the bottom of each soup bowl. Ladle in the soup and squeeze some fresh lemon juice on top. As a finishing touch, drizzle a little extra virgin olive oil on top.

ESCAROLE AND CANNELLINI BEAN SOUP

Serves 4 to 6

Escarole and Cannellini Bean Soup is a classic and typical southern Italian soup dating back to *cucina povera*, the tradition of frugal peasant cooking. I was a picky eater as a young girl. When my grandfather or mother proposed to make this soup, I turned up my nose. As an adult, I have grown to enjoy more and more traditional dishes of my childhood. Often, I am asked by students what I do with escarole; I always suggest this nutritious and comforting soup. Especially when eaten in good company, it warms the stomach and the heart.

2 to 3 tablespoons extra virgin olive oil
1 large red onion, thinly sliced
1 stalk celery, diced
1 carrot, peeled and diced
2 cloves garlic, thinly sliced
1 pound escarole, roughly chopped
Kosher salt
Freshly ground black pepper
8 cups chicken or vegetable broth
1 cup cooked and drained dried cannellini beans or drained canned beans
2 to 3 tablespoons chopped fresh Italian parsley leaves
Grated pecorino or Parmesan

In a large saucepot, heat the oil over medium heat. Add the onions, celery, and carrots, and sauté until the onions are translucent, 4 to 5 minutes. Add the garlic and sauté another minute. Next, add the escarole, and sauté for 6 to 8 minutes. Season with salt and pepper.

Add the broth and bring to a boil. Cover, reduce heat to low, and simmer about 20 minutes, then add the beans. Replace the cover, and simmer until the vegetables are just tender, 10 to 15 minutes. Remove from heat. Transfer to a serving bowl, and sprinkle with chopped parsley and grated cheese.

Tip: *To cook dried cannellini beans: Pour dried cannellini beans into a colander and remove any pebbles or shriveled beans. Hold the colander of dried beans under running cold water to remove any dust from the beans. Place the dried cannellini beans in a large bowl with water to completely submerge the beans. Cover and leave the beans to soak overnight in the refrigerator to rehydrate. Pour the soaked beans into a colander over a sink and rinse with cold water. In a medium pot, boil the cannellini beans in fresh water to cover over medium heat until tender, about 1 hour. Drain, and they are ready to use.*

FISH AND FENNEL SOUP
Serves 4 to 6

This is another artful soup from the *cucina povera*. Fishermen made this soup from the fish left over at the fishermen's market after selling their catch of the day. They would cook the leftover fish or scraps of fish with fennel. With a few added ingredients from the pantry, this soup stands out from the rest. In fact, today it is considered a gourmet dish.

2 pounds tilapia, sole, cod, or flounder fillets
2 to 3 tablespoons extra virgin olive oil
2 large sweet onions, thinly sliced
4 cloves garlic, minced
1 (28-ounce) can plum tomatoes, drained and crushed into small pieces
1 large fennel bulb, cut into small cubes, feathery greens reserved for garnish
30 large pitted green olives, crushed with the heel of your hand
½ cup golden raisins
1 pinch saffron threads, steeped in 2 tablespoons warm broth or water
3 to 4 tablespoons minced fresh Italian parsley leaves
¼ teaspoon kosher salt
¼ teaspoon freshly ground black pepper
6 cups vegetable or fish broth
1 lemon

Clean the fish fillets, pat dry with paper towels, and cut them into bite-size pieces.

Heat the oil in a large heavy-bottomed skillet over medium heat. Add the onions, and sauté until translucent, 6 to 8 minutes. Add the garlic and sauté until barely golden. Add the crushed tomatoes; sauté for about 5 minutes. Stir in the fennel, olives, raisins, saffron, parsley, salt, and pepper. Sauté for 2 to 3 minutes.

Add the broth and bring to a boil. Reduce heat to medium-low. Add the fish, partially cover the pot, and simmer until the fish is fully cooked, about 10 minutes. Serve in bowls, topped with fresh fennel greens and a squeeze of lemon juice.

ONION, CELERY, AND COUSCOUS SOUP

Serves 4 to 6

Called *hsou*, this is a classic and traditional Tunisian soup particularly famous for its spicy flavors. Muslims usually prepare it during Ramadan, the period of fasting. It is served in the evening with fresh milk and dates. The original recipe is made with rue leaves; since rue is difficult to find, I do not include it. Rich in flavors of caraway, paprika, and coriander, this is a soup that you must taste.

- 3 to 4 tablespoons extra virgin olive oil
- 1 large sweet onion, minced
- 3 cloves garlic, crushed
- 1 tablespoon tomato paste
- 1 teaspoon ground caraway seeds
- 1 teaspoon ground coriander
- 1 teaspoon paprika
- 1 teaspoon Harissa (page 188)
- ½ teaspoon kosher salt
- ¼ teaspoon freshly ground black pepper
- 1 stalk celery with leaves, minced
- 4 cups hot vegetable broth or water
- ½ cup dry couscous
- 1 lemon, peeled, seeds removed, finely minced
- 5 to 10 fresh Italian parsley leaves

Heat the oil in a large saucepot over medium heat. Add the onions and sauté until translucent, 6 to 8 minutes. Add the garlic and sauté about 1 minute.

Stir in the tomato paste, caraway, coriander, paprika, Harissa, salt, and pepper. Reduce heat to medium-low and cook, stirring continually, for 2 to 3 minutes. Add the celery and sauté about 3 minutes.

Add the broth and stir well. Bring to a boil over medium-high heat. Add the couscous and stir well again. Reduce heat to low, cover, and cook until the couscous is tender, about 10 minutes.

Add the lemon flesh to the soup. Taste, and adjust seasoning if necessary. Warm for 5 more minutes and remove from the heat. Transfer to serving bowls; top with parsley leaves.

PUMPKIN AND DITALINI SOUP

Serves 4 to 6

On a cold winter evening, there is nothing better to warm up with than a delicious thick pumpkin and pasta soup. Children, as well as adults, love ditalini because it is small and easy to eat. I add some Maghrebi spices to make this soup my own.

2 to 3 tablespoons extra virgin olive oil
1 sweet onion, minced
1 pound pumpkin, peeled, seeded, and cut in ½-inch cubes
8 cups warm water
1 pinch red pepper flakes
½ teaspoon ground coriander
½ teaspoon ground cumin
2 bay leaves
Kosher salt
1½ cups ditalini pasta
¼ cup grated Parmesan

In a large saucepan, heat the oil over medium heat. Add the onions and sauté until translucent and golden, 6 to 8 minutes. Add the pumpkin and sauté about 5 minutes. Add the warm water, red pepper flakes, coriander, cumin, and bay leaves. Season with salt. Mix well and bring to a boil.

Reduce heat to medium-low and continue cooking until the pumpkin is almost tender. Remove and discard the bay leaves. Add the ditalini and cook until tender, about 15 minutes, stirring occasionally. Continue cooking until the pumpkin becomes a puree. Ladle into soup bowls and sprinkle with Parmesan.

SPICY CAULIFLOWER SOUP

Serves 4 to 6

I still have memories of being in the kitchen helping my grandfather while he made this *minestra*. I was always in charge of breaking up spaghetti to the size of very tiny pasta. We used the broken spaghetti as the pastina for many of our *minestri*—it was an important task for me. How proud I was to be the assistant cook at that young age!

This easy-to-prepare soup will be appreciated even by those who don't love cauliflower. With the addition of the spices and the pastina, it's a robust dish.

2 to 3 tablespoons extra virgin olive oil
1 red onion, diced
3 cloves garlic, minced
1 cup tomato puree
¼ to ½ teaspoon Harissa (page 188)
1 teaspoon ground cumin
1 teaspoon ground coriander
1 large head cauliflower, cut into florets
8 cups hot vegetable broth
Kosher salt
1½ cups pastina or orzo
2 to 3 tablespoons torn fresh mint leaves

Heat the oil in a large saucepan over medium heat. Add the onions and sauté until translucent and golden, 6 to 8 minutes. Add the garlic and sauté until fragrant, about 1 minute. Next, stir in the tomato puree, Harissa, cumin, and coriander. Sauté for 2 minutes.

Add the cauliflower and sauté 2 to 3 minutes. Add the broth and bring to a boil. Reduce heat to medium-low, and simmer until the cauliflower is tender, 5 to 8 minutes. Taste for seasoning and add salt if needed.

Add the pastina and cook until al dente, according to the package directions. When ready, transfer to soup bowls, and top with fresh mint.

VELVETY CHICKPEA AND PASTA SOUP

Serves 4

This simple *minestra* was usually served in the wintertime even though we had very mild winters. It reminds me of the days when my grandmother and mother prepared it—it was quite a ritual. The chickpeas needed to soak overnight to be used the next day. Then they would boil the chickpeas before making the *minestra*. Today, the *minestra* can be more quickly prepared using canned chickpeas, draining them well before using them. I make this soup at home, regardless of the season, when I have a yearning for a favorite childhood food to bring back memories of my being in the kitchen with my mother and grandmother.

2 tablespoons extra virgin olive oil, plus more for drizzling
2 cloves garlic, minced
1 tablespoon minced fresh rosemary leaves
2 tablespoons tomato paste
4 cups cooked chickpeas or drained canned chickpeas
3 cups chicken or vegetable broth, divided
½ teaspoon ground cumin
½ teaspoon ground coriander
1 pinch red pepper flakes
Kosher salt
Freshly ground black pepper
1 cup ditalini pasta

Heat the oil in a large saucepot over medium-low heat. Add the garlic and rosemary and sauté until the garlic is fragrant, about 30 seconds. Make a well in the middle of the pan. Add the tomato paste to the middle of the pan. Increase the heat to medium, and sauté, undisturbed, for 2 minutes. Occasionally stir the garlic and rosemary to prevent them from burning. Add the chickpeas, 1 cup broth, cumin, coriander, and red pepper flakes. Season with salt and pepper. Mix well. Cook for 5 minutes, remove from the heat, and cool slightly.

Transfer to a food processor, or use an immersion blender, and blend until the mixture is creamy and homogenized. Return the mixture to the pot; add ½ to 2 cups of the remaining broth, depending on how thick you like your soup. Keep warm until the pasta is added.

In the meantime, in a separate pot, cook the ditalini in salted boiling water until al dente according to the package directions. When ready, drain, and transfer the ditalini to the pot of soup. Stir to combine. Ladle the soup into individual bowls, and drizzle some oil over the top. Serve warm.

Note: *Any leftover soup can be refrigerated and reheated. The soup will thicken up in the refrigerator; you may need to add some broth or water when you reheat it.*

BREAD SOUP

Serves 4 to 6

*L*a cucina povera, "the poor kitchen," originated centuries ago. It was food made by peasants or poor people. Because those people could not afford to purchase many ingredients, they came up with imaginative, artful ways of cooking the same ingredients in a variety of ways. Many gastronomic discoveries were probably made a bit by accident, with a little imagination, and of course, out of necessity.

"*Pancotto*", which means "cooked bread" in Italian, is a simple dish from the *cucina povera* cuisine in which throwing away leftover bread is considered a sacrilege. *Pancotto* was a dish to fill hungry bellies. My mother often fed *pancotto* to my younger brother when he was a toddler. There was little money for meats, vegetables, and fruits, so my little brother had boiled bread instead of milk. The *pancotto* is an old recipe, but I think it will continue to be prepared for hundreds of years to come.

    2 to 3 tablespoons extra virgin olive oil
    4 cloves garlic, thinly sliced
    1 pinch red pepper flakes
    1 (28-ounce) can whole plum tomatoes, with juice, finely chopped
    8 cups vegetable broth or water
    2 whole bay leaves
    Kosher salt
    Freshly ground black pepper
    2 cups ¼-inch cubes day-old bread
    2 tablespoons torn fresh mint leaves
    Freshly grated Parmesan, for serving

In a large soup pot, heat the oil over medium heat. Add the garlic and red pepper flakes and cook just until the garlic is golden, about 1 minute. Stir in the tomatoes and their juice, cover, and cook for 3 to 5 minutes. Add the broth and bay leaves. Season with salt and pepper. Bring the soup to a boil.

Add the bread cubes and reduce the heat to low. Cook for a few minutes: the bread will warm up, soak up some of the broth, and thicken the soup. Remove and discard the bay leaves. Transfer the soup to serving bowls, top with mint and grated Parmesan.

PASTA

EASY PASTA DISHES

Linguine Milanese
Fettuccine with Lemon and Arugula
Linguine with Mussels, Capers, and Tomatoes
Spaghetti with Raw Tomato Sauce
Orzo with Carrots, Onions, and Marsala Wine
Pasta alla Scarpara
Pasta with Aromatic Herbs
Pasta with Fennel and Almonds
Pasta with Zucchini and Mint
Pasta with Ricotta and Dill Pesto
Pasta with Sausage and Cauliflower
Pasta with Tomatoes and Golden Bread Crumbs
Pasta with Tuna and Tomato Sauce

BAKED PASTA
(PASTA AL FORNO)

Neapolitan Lasagna with Mini Meatballs
Sicilian Pasta and Eggplant Timballo

HOW TO PROPERLY COOK PASTA

Cooking pasta correctly is not too difficult. There are, however, some fundamental pasta-cooking rules. We begin by choosing the right pot, deep enough and wide enough to hold a sufficient quantity of water. Pasta needs a constant temperature; it is easier to maintain that temperature with a large amount of water. The pasta cooking time will depend both on its shape and its thickness.

SOME ITALIAN PASTA RULES:

- Use 1 gallon of water for each pound of pasta.

- Use 2 tablespoons of kosher salt for each gallon of water.

- Add oil to the water only when a recipe calls for it, otherwise it is not necessary.

- Water must be at a full bubbling boil before adding the pasta. Pasta added to the water before it starts to boil could turn out mushy.

- Put the pasta in the pot all at once.

- Cook the pasta uncovered, at a fast boil so that the temperature stays uniform.

- Stir vigorously for the first 45 seconds so the pasta does not stick.

- For cooking time, follow the directions on the pasta box. If you are unsure what al dente should be, taste the pasta as many times as you need until it's the right consistency for you. Reserve a cup of pasta water, if needed, for the sauce.

- Never rinse the pasta unless it is for a pasta salad or if a recipe requires it.

- Pasta sauce should add flavor to the dish without hiding the original flavor of the pasta, so do not over sauce.

- When you are going to bake the pasta, boil it for few minutes less, because it will continue to cook while baking. Add a little more sauce to the pasta than you normally would because the pasta will absorb more sauce when it is in the oven.

Flavors of the Maghreb and Southern Italy

WHAT IS A GOOD PASTA TO BUY?

Read the label when purchasing dry pasta. The best quality pasta is made of 100 percent semolina (durum wheat semolina). Pasta made from durum wheat retains its shape and firmness while cooking. When cooked properly, it will not get mushy or gummy. Pasta that is not made with semolina will produce a softer noodle and will not hold up well when tossing.

COMMONLY USED PASTA:

You can use them interchangeably within each category:

Long Pasta: capellini, linguini, spaghetti, thin linguini, thin spaghetti

Flat Pasta: fettuccini, parpadelle, tagliatelle

Short Pasta: farfalle, fusilli, mini penne, penne, rigatoni, ziti

PASTA SAUCE AND PAIRING GUIDE

In general, long pasta requires a runny sauce. This type of pasta tends to dry quickly, so reserve some cooking pasta water to add to the sauce. Short pasta requires rich and dense sauces because this pasta needs to mix well with the sauce. Cook it for a minute or two longer in the pan, together with its sauce, on medium heat.

BASIC MARINARA SAUCE
Makes about 6 cups

Marinara sauce got its name from sailors (*marinai*) who often prepared it because it was quick and easy to make on a ship. *Spaghetti alla marinara* originated in Naples, Italy. Marinara sauce is used on top of pasta and pizza. It is typically prepared to cook fish and seafood in, just as the sailors did. I make and use this marinara sauce over and over again for a variety of dishes. Whenever I have any left in my dish, I scoop it up with bread, and clean up my plate!

1 ½ cups minced sweet onion
3 tablespoons extra virgin olive oil
4 to 5 cloves garlic, minced
1 tablespoon granulated sugar
1 teaspoon dried oregano leaves
1 (28-ounce) can San Marzano peeled tomatoes, with juice, crushed
2 tablespoons torn fresh basil leaves
Kosher salt
Freshly ground black pepper
2 tablespoons tomato paste
1 ½ cups vegetable or chicken broth

Heat a large skillet over medium heat. Add the onions and sauté without oil until the liquid from the onions has reduced, 3 to 4 minutes. Add the oil and continue to sauté the onions until golden, 6 to 8 minutes. Add the garlic and cook until fragrant, about 1 minute. Add the sugar, oregano, tomatoes with their juice, and basil. Season with salt and pepper. Mix well and cook for 10 to 15 minutes. Add the tomato paste and broth; mix well. Cover and cook, stirring occasionally, until the sauce thickens, about 10 minutes.

Tip: *Here's a method of cooking onions that I created in my early teens; it really enhances the flavor of the onions. I place the cut onions into a skillet without oil first. Once most of the liquid has evaporated, I add the oil. I find that while the onion is cooking in a dry pan, the liquid goes to the bottom of the pan and evaporates. Once the oil hits the pan, that wonderful residue from the onions gets mixed with the onions and oil.*

QUICK MEAT SAUCE

Makes about 3 cups

There are many versions of quick meat sauce in Italy, dictated by region and family tradition. I teach this sauce in my cooking classes. My students have told me they make it often at home because they find it tasty and easy to make. This versatile sauce can be served in short pasta dishes, lasagna, or other baked pasta dishes.

2 tablespoons extra virgin olive oil
2 ounces diced pancetta
6 ounces lean ground beef
6 ounces ground Italian sausage
1 large sweet onion, minced
3 large cloves garlic, minced
1 large carrot, peeled and minced
1 pinch red pepper flakes
Kosher salt
Freshly ground black pepper
1 cup canned Italian tomato puree
½ cup dry red wine or Marsala wine
½ cup chicken or vegetable broth
2 tablespoons chopped fresh Italian parsley leaves

Heat a large skillet over medium heat. Add the oil and pancetta; cook until the pancetta is crisp, 3 to 4 minutes. Add the ground beef and sausage. Cook, making sure that the meat begins releasing its juices, until the meat is cooked through and browned and all of the liquid has evaporated, 8 to 10 minutes. Add the onions, garlic, and carrot; cook until onions are translucent and just golden, 6 to 8 minutes. Add the red pepper flakes, and season with salt and pepper.

Stir in the tomato puree and cook for 2 to 3 minutes. Add the wine, broth, and parsley; stir well and bring to a boil. Reduce heat to low. Cover and simmer for 10 to 12 minutes.

PESTO

Pesto, dating back to the second half of the nineteenth century, is one of the most famous and appreciated of the Italian *crudo* (raw) sauces. "Pesto" is derived from the Italian verb "*pestare*," which is the act of grinding or crushing. "Pesto" also refers to the ancient method of grinding or crushing food with a pestle in a mortar, a method still used today. The traditional pesto sauce, *Pesto alla Genovese*, was created in Genoa in the Liguria region of Northern Italy. It is a fragrant sauce that perfectly combines garlic, fresh basil, pine nuts, a mix of Parmigiano-Reggiano and Fiore Sardo (from sheep's milk) cheeses, and extra virgin olive oil. Pecorino Romano is often used instead of Fiore Sardo. The pesto's preparation is very simple: Add a pinch of salt, peeled garlic, and fresh basil leaves to the mortar, then crush it all together with the pestle by pressing and twisting. Then add the pine nuts and crush them into the paste. Add in the Parmesan; drizzle in the oil; stir until you have a creamy sauce.

Recently, pesto sauces have evolved to include other combinations of ingredients including herbs such as dill, parsley, and mint; nuts such as pistachios and almonds; even spinach, arugula, and other greens. It is still a simple recipe made with limited ingredients. For those who do not want to use a mortar and pestle, the technique can be simplified with the use of a blender or a food processor.

Pesto should be stored covered with a layer of extra-virgin olive oil on top to keep it from spoiling. Keep it in a tightly covered jar in the refrigerator; it can last up to a week. It can also be frozen without adding oil to the top.

Although I am a big fan of tradition, I am offering you some pesto variations that I have made for my family and in my cooking classes. All have received rave reviews. I still use my large pestle and mortar to keep the tradition going even during my cooking lessons.

USES FOR PESTO

Use pesto sauce with pasta, grilled fish or seafood, potato salad, dips, instead of mayonnaise in sandwiches, with eggs, frittatas, vegetables—use your imagination!

HOW TO MAKE
PROPER PESTO

- Water is pesto's enemy. Rinse and completely dry all herbs, greens, and other fresh ingredients. Any residue of water will change the flavor, texture, and sometimes even the color of the pesto.

- Roughly chop all ingredients ahead of time to make it easier to pulse them in the food processor.

- Have all the ingredients ready before you start.

- Place all the ingredients in a food processor; pulse a few times. If the mixture is sticking to the bottom, remove the lid and mix well with a scraper. Pulse again until you have the consistency you prefer. Some people like pesto slightly smooth, very smooth, a little chunky, or very chunky.

- Be sure to taste the pesto before removing it from the food processor. If you feel you'd like more garlic, cheese, or seasoning, add a little at a time until you achieve the flavor you like. If you have too much garlic or cheese, just add a little more of the herbs to balance it.

- If you are not going to use the pesto immediately, transfer it to a small glass bowl or jar. Immediately add olive oil on top so the pesto does not discolor. Be sure to cover the entire top of the pesto. Cover tightly and store in the refrigerator for up to one week. If you do not use all of the pesto at one time and you have some left over, top with olive oil again, cover, and refrigerate.

- Pesto can be made with a variety of nuts; experiment to see what you like best. You can use hazelnuts, almonds, pine nuts, walnuts, or pistachios.

AROMATIC FRESH HERBS AND ROSEWATER PESTO

Makes about 1 ¼ cups

Note: *Water is pesto's enemy. Rinse and completely dry all herbs, greens, and other fresh ingredients. Any residue of water will change the flavor, texture, and sometimes, even the color of the pesto.*

½ cup roughly torn fresh basil leaves
½ cup roughly chopped fresh Italian parsley leaves
½ cup roughly chopped fresh tarragon leaves
½ cup roughly chopped fresh dill
2 tablespoons chopped scallions
⅓ cup grated Parmesan
½ cup whole hazelnuts, lightly toasted
1 teaspoon rosewater
Kosher salt
Freshly ground white pepper
½ cup extra virgin olive oil

Place the basil, parsley, tarragon, dill, scallions, Parmesan, hazelnuts, and rosewater in a food processor. Season with salt and pepper; pulse a few times until everything is well blended. Drizzle in the oil and pulse a few times to emulsify. Taste for seasoning and adjust if needed.

ARTICHOKE PESTO

Makes about 1 ½ cups

Note: *Water is pesto's enemy. Rinse and completely dry all herbs, greens, and other fresh ingredients. Any residue of water will change the flavor, texture, and sometimes, even the color of the pesto.*

2 cups jarred artichoke hearts in water, drained
1 cup torn fresh basil leaves
½ cup slivered almonds, lightly toasted
Zest of 1 lemon
Kosher salt
Freshly ground black pepper
⅓ cup extra virgin olive oil

Place the artichokes, basil, almonds, and lemon zest in a food processor, and season with salt and pepper; pulse a few times until everything is well blended. Drizzle in the oil and pulse a few times to emulsify. Taste for seasoning and adjust if needed.

ARUGULA PESTO

Makes about 1 ¼ cups

Note: *Water is pesto's enemy. Rinse and completely dry all herbs, greens, and other fresh ingredients. Any residue of water will change the flavor, texture, and sometimes, even the color of the pesto.*

2 cups roughly chopped arugula
2 cloves garlic, roughly chopped
½ cup chopped walnuts, lightly toasted
1 tablespoon fresh lemon juice
⅓ cup grated Parmesan
¼ teaspoon red pepper flakes
½ cup extra virgin olive oil

Place the arugula, garlic, walnuts, lemon juice, Parmesan, and red pepper flakes in a food processor, and pulse a few times until everything is well blended. Drizzle in the oil and pulse a few times to emulsify. Taste for seasoning and adjust if needed.

PISTACHIO MINT PESTO
Makes about 1 cup

Note: *Water is pesto's enemy. Rinse and completely dry all herbs, greens, and other fresh ingredients. Any residue of water will change the flavor, texture, and sometimes, even the color of the pesto.*

1 cup shelled pistachios, lightly toasted
2 cloves garlic, roughly chopped
1 cup torn fresh basil leaves
1 cup torn fresh mint leaves
Kosher salt
Freshly ground black pepper
½ cup extra virgin olive oil

Place the pistachios, garlic, basil, and mint in a food processor. Season with salt and pepper; pulse a few times until everything is well blended. Drizzle in the oil and pulse a few times to emulsify. Taste for seasoning and adjust if needed.

BELL PEPPER PESTO
Makes about 1 cup

Note: *Water is pesto's enemy. Rinse and completely dry all herbs, greens, and other fresh ingredients. Any residue of water will change the flavor, texture, and sometimes, even the color of the pesto.*

1 large orange bell pepper, ribs and seeds removed, roughly chopped
1 large red bell pepper, ribs and seeds removed, roughly chopped
2 cloves garlic, roughly chopped
1 cup roughly torn fresh basil leaves
¼ teaspoon roughly chopped fresh oregano leaves
½ cup blanched almonds, lightly toasted
½ cup grated Parmesan
Kosher salt
Freshly ground black pepper
⅓ cup extra virgin olive oil

Place peppers, garlic, basil, oregano, almonds, and Parmesan in a food processor. Season with salt and pepper; pulse a few times until everything is well blended. Drizzle in the oil and pulse a few times to emulsify. Taste for seasoning and adjust if needed.

SICILIAN ANCHOVY PESTO

Makes about ¾ cup

Note: *Water is pesto's enemy. Rinse and completely dry all herbs, greens, and other fresh ingredients. Any residue of water will change the flavor, texture, and sometimes, even the color of the pesto.*

4 anchovies, packed in oil, drained
10 oil-packed sundried tomatoes, drained
2 cloves garlic, roughly chopped
½ cup pine nuts, lightly toasted
2 tablespoons roughly torn fresh basil leaves
1 teaspoon chopped fresh thyme leaves
¼ teaspoon red pepper flakes
⅓ cup extra virgin olive oil
Kosher salt

Place anchovies, tomatoes, garlic, pine nuts, basil, thyme, and red pepper flakes in a food processor, and pulse a few times until everything is well blended. Drizzle in the oil and pulse a few times—the pesto should be chunky. Taste for seasoning; add salt and adjust other flavors if needed.

SUNDRIED TOMATO AND OLIVE PESTO

Makes about 1¼ cups

Note: *Water is pesto's enemy. Rinse and completely dry all herbs, greens, and other fresh ingredients. Any residue of water will change the flavor, texture, and sometimes, even the color of the pesto.*

10 sundried tomatoes in oil, drained
3 cloves garlic, roughly chopped
20 pitted black olives
½ cup slivered almonds, lightly toasted
2 tablespoons chopped fresh rosemary leaves
½ teaspoon red pepper flakes
2 teaspoons balsamic vinegar
Kosher salt
Freshly ground black pepper
½ cup extra virgin olive oil

Place sundried tomatoes, garlic, olives, almonds, rosemary, red pepper flakes, and vinegar in a food processor. Season with salt and pepper. Pulse a few times until everything is well blended. Drizzle in the oil; pulse a few times to emulsify. Taste for seasoning and adjust if needed.

EASY PASTA DISHES

LINGUINE MILANESE

Serves 4 to 6

We did not eat meat on Fridays because of our religious beliefs. I remember eating this pasta a few times a month on Fridays. I knew when I smelled dill boiling, that evening there was going to be Milanese at the table. I loved to hear the sizzle of the hot bread crumbs when my mom sprinkled them over the pasta. If you want to hear that sizzle, be sure to cook the bread crumbs at the last moment so they will still be hot when you sprinkle them over your pasta.

FOR THE SAUCE:
1 bunch fresh dill with about 2 inches of the stems, roughly chopped
Kosher salt
3 to 4 tablespoons extra virgin olive oil
3 cloves garlic, minced
1 (28-ounce) can tomato puree
1 tablespoon granulated sugar, optional
½ teaspoon freshly ground black pepper

FOR THE PASTA:
1 pound linguine
Kosher salt

FOR THE TOPPING:
2 tablespoons extra virgin olive oil
1½ cups dry Italian bread crumbs

To make the sauce:

Place the dill in a small saucepan, add water to cover and 1 teaspoon salt. Bring to a boil and cook the dill for about 10 minutes. Reserve 1 cup of the dill water, drain the dill, and set both aside separately.

Heat a large skillet over medium heat. Add the oil and garlic, and sauté until the garlic is barely golden, about 1 minute. Very carefully add the tomato puree; it may spatter. Add the sugar, if using, ½ teaspoon salt, and the pepper; sauté until the sauce is thick, 6 to 8 minutes. Stir in the dill and ½ cup of the reserved dill water to the sauce, bring to a boil, and then reduce the heat to low. Simmer for 15 to 18 minutes. If the sauce appears too thick, stir in a little more of the reserved dill water, a few tablespoons at a time.

To cook the linguine:

Heat a 5- to 6-quart pot of water over high heat and bring to a boil. Add the linguine and 2 tablespoons salt and bring to a second boil. Stir vigorously for the first 45 seconds so the linguine will not stick. Cook the linguine until al dente according to the package directions.

While the linguine is cooking, make the topping.

To make the topping:

In a small skillet, heat the oil over medium-low heat. Add the bread crumbs and cook, stirring frequently, until the mixture is well toasted and golden, 5 to 8 minutes. Remove from the skillet quickly so that the bread crumbs will not burn. Transfer to a small bowl.

Assembly:

When the linguine is ready, drain it, and transfer it to a large serving bowl. Fold in 1 cup of the sauce. Place the linguine in individual bowls with more sauce on top. Sprinkle on the toasted hot bread crumbs, and serve.

FETTUCCINE WITH LEMON AND ARUGULA

Serves 4 to 6

For an impromptu lunch or dinner with friends, I want to prepare the fastest, easiest, and freshest dish I can so I can spend more time with my friends and not so much time in the kitchen. Fresh lemon juice, lemon zest, and pungent arugula make this pasta a winner every time. I have made this dish in several cooking classes; I always enjoy my students' silent enjoyment as they sample it.

2 large lemons
1 pound fettuccine
Kosher salt
4 to 6 tablespoons extra virgin olive oil
2 cloves garlic, finely minced
12 to 14 large fresh basil leaves, in chiffonade
1 pinch red pepper flakes
Freshly ground black pepper
2 cups baby arugula
½ cup grated Parmesan

Zest the 2 lemons into a small bowl. Set aside.

Heat a 5- to 6-quart pot of water over high heat and bring to a boil. Add the fettucine and 2 tablespoons salt and bring to a second boil. Stir vigorously for the first 45 seconds so the fettuccine will not stick. About 5 minutes after the water has boiled, squeeze the juice of 1 lemon into the pot; reserve the remaining lemon for another recipe. This will flavor the pasta and pasta water. Cook the fettuccine until al dente according to the package directions.

While the pasta is cooking, heat a large skillet over medium heat. Add the oil and garlic, and sauté until the garlic is barely golden, about 1 minute. Add the basil, all of the lemon zest, and the red pepper flakes. Season with salt and pepper. Cook for about 1 minute. Add the arugula, toss, and sauté just to warm through, about 2 minutes. Do not cook the arugula; it will be somewhat wilted.

When the fettuccine is ready, reserve 1 cup of the hot pasta water. Drain the fettuccine and transfer it to the skillet with the sauce. Toss well to coat. If there is not enough sauce, add the reserved pasta water a little at a time. Remove from heat and top with the grated Parmesan. Serve hot.

LINGUINE WITH MUSSELS, CAPERS, AND TOMATOES

Serves 4 to 6

This pasta sauce originated in the Campania region of Italy, where I was born. When we immigrated to the United States, each summer we would go to the beach for a week's vacation. My father would look for a place on the beach with lots of big rocks. There, we would climb down and remove the mussels from the rocks. Then we would put the mussels in a small bucket to take them back to the beach house where my mother would cook up a pot of pasta and mussels for us.

1 pound mussels, cleaned and debearded
1 pound linguine
Kosher salt
3 to 4 tablespoons extra virgin olive oil, plus more for drizzling
5 to 6 cloves garlic, thinly sliced
3 to 4 tablespoons chopped Italian parsley leaves, plus more for serving
½ to 1 teaspoon red pepper flakes
2 tablespoons capers in brine, drained
1 teaspoon dried oregano leaves
Freshly ground black pepper
2 pints fresh grape tomatoes, halved
½ cup dry white wine

Check to make sure that all the mussels are closed. Discard any mussels that are open or have open cracks; they are not edible.

Heat a 5- to 6-quart pot of water over high heat and bring to a boil. Add the linguine and 2 tablespoons salt and bring to a second boil. Stir vigorously for the first 45 seconds so the linguine will not stick. Cook the linguine until al dente according to the package directions.

Heat a large skillet over medium heat. Add the oil and garlic, and sauté until the garlic is barely golden, about 1 minute. Add the parsley, red pepper flakes, capers, and oregano. Season with salt and pepper. Cook for about 1 minute. Add the tomatoes and cook just until they are turning soft but still hold their shape, 5 to 6 minutes. Increase the heat to medium-high, add the mussels, and mix well with the sauce. Add the wine, cover, and cook until the mussels have opened, 6 to 8 minutes. Remove from the heat and discard any mussels that remain closed; they are not edible.

When the linguine is ready, reserve ½ cup of hot pasta water. Drain the linguine, and transfer to the skillet with the sauce and mussels. Toss well to coat. If the sauce is too thick, add the reserved pasta water a little at a time, until it is the consistency you desire. Serve hot with extra parsley and pepper, and a drizzle of olive oil if desired.

SPAGHETTI WITH RAW TOMATO SAUCE

Serves 4 to 6

Another memory of a meatless Friday meal. I was allowed to help make this spaghetti dish when I was a child because there was no cooking involved. It was exciting to squish the tomatoes with my hands. I felt like a big girl helping to make the sauce. Now that my parents and grandparents are no longer around, my brothers always ask me if I could make this pasta sauce for them and their kids when they come over. My older brother, Adriano, says that every time I make it, it reminds him of when we were kids in my mother's kitchen. It makes him happy and sad at the same time to remember the old days.

1 pound spaghetti
Kosher salt
1 (28-ounce) can San Marzano tomatoes, with juice, finely crushed
1 small red onion, very thinly sliced
15 to 20 pitted green olives, roughly chopped
20 capers in brine, drained and roughly chopped
2 to 3 cloves garlic, minced
Freshly ground black pepper
½ cup extra virgin olive oil
Freshly shaved Parmesan
¼ cup roughly torn fresh basil leaves, plus extra for garnish
3 to 4 tablespoons roughly chopped fresh Italian parsley leaves

Heat a 5- to 6-quart pot of water over high heat and bring to a boil. Add the spaghetti and 2 tablespoons salt and bring to a second boil. Stir vigorously for the first 45 seconds so the spaghetti will not stick. Cook the spaghetti until al dente according to the package directions.

While the spaghetti is cooking, prepare the sauce: In a large bowl, combine the tomatoes with their juice, onions, olives, capers, and garlic. Season with salt and pepper. Add the oil and mix gently. Taste for seasonings and adjust as needed. Add the parsley and basil and mix well.

When the spaghetti is ready, drain it, and transfer it to the bowl with the sauce, toss well to coat. Sprinkle with shaved Parmesan and basil and parsley leaves and serve.

ORZO WITH CARROTS, ONIONS, AND MARSALA WINE

Serves 4 to 6

Marsala is a semidry wine rich with aromas of toasted almonds, dried fruit, citrus, vanilla, caramel, and honey. Marsala is somewhat different from other wines because of its bouquet and flavor, which complement the rest of the ingredients in this dish. This orzo is a first course or side to serve with meat, fish, or seafood. If you serve it as a first course pasta dish, please fill up your bowl to the top, and add more grated cheese. I promise you will know what I mean when you taste it!

3 cups orzo
Kosher salt
3 tablespoons extra virgin olive oil
1 large red onion, minced
2 stalks celery with leaves, minced
2 carrots, peeled and minced
Freshly ground black pepper
¼ cup Marsala wine
2 to 3 tablespoons torn fresh basil leaves
Freshly grated Parmesan

Fill a 5- to 6-quart pot about three-quarters full of water. Bring to a boil over high heat. Add the orzo and 2 tablespoons salt and bring to a second boil. Stir vigorously for the first 45 seconds, so the orzo will not stick. Cook the orzo until al dente according to the package directions.

Heat the oil in a large skillet over medium heat. Add the onions, celery, and carrots, and cook, stirring occasionally, until tender and just golden, 8 to 10 minutes. Season with salt and pepper. Stir in the Marsala wine and cook for another minute.

When the orzo is ready, drain it, and transfer it to the skillet with the sauce. Toss well to coat. Remove from the heat and scatter the basil on top. Serve hot, topped with the Parmesan.

Pasta alla Scarpara

Serves 4 to 6

My grandfather sometimes made this sauce for me because it was a good alternative to the usual pasta with tomato sauce. *Pasta alla Scarpara*, in its extreme simplicity, is a delicious and very easy-to-prepare sauce. Of course, it is very tasty on pasta, but it is an excellent condiment on fish and seafood also.

1 pound penne
Kosher salt
1 large sweet onion, minced
3 tablespoons extra virgin olive oil, plus more for drizzling
3 cloves garlic, thinly sliced
3 tablespoons chopped fresh Italian parsley leaves, plus more for garnish
3 tablespoons torn fresh basil leaves, plus more for garnish
4 to 5 jarred sundried tomatoes in oil, drained and diced
1 pinch red pepper flakes
Freshly ground black pepper
2 pints fresh grape or cherry tomatoes, halved
1 tablespoon tomato paste
4 tablespoons dry white wine
½ cup grated Parmesan

Heat a 5- to 6-quart pot of water over high heat and bring to a boil. Add the penne and 2 tablespoons salt and bring to a second boil. Stir vigorously for the first 45 seconds so the penne will not stick. Cook the penne until al dente according to the package directions.

Heat a large skillet over medium heat. Add the onions and sauté without oil until the liquid from the onions has reduced, 3 to 4 minutes. Add the oil and continue to sauté the onions until golden, 6 to 8 minutes. Add the garlic and sauté for 1 minute. Add parsley, basil, and sundried tomatoes; cook for 2 to 3 minutes. Add the red pepper flakes, and season with salt and pepper. Stir together.

Add the fresh tomatoes to the skillet and cook 5 to 7 minutes. Make a little indentation or well in the middle of the skillet, pushing all the other ingredients to the sides, and add the tomato paste. Drizzle a drop or two of olive oil on the tomato paste and cook for 2 to 3 minutes, stirring occasionally. This process will help caramelize the flavors of the tomato paste, and it will become very tasty. Add the white wine and stir. Cook until most of the wine has reduced, about 5 minutes.

When the penne is ready, drain it, and transfer it to the skillet with the sauce. Toss well to coat the pasta. Serve warm topped with the Parmesan and some basil and parsley.

Tip: *Take a few extra minutes to cook the tomato paste in the middle of the pan because it caramelizes the paste and intensifies the flavors. I learned this method from my aunt many years ago. You could skip this step and just mix the tomato paste in, but it won't be as tasty!*

Pasta with Aromatic Herbs

Serves 4 to 6

Just imagine using your favorite herbs from your garden and combining them with some light seasoning and good olive oil to create this pasta dish. Once the herbs hit the butter and olive oil in the skillet, a wonderful aroma fills the room. When you fold this aromatic sauce into the pasta, you create the freshest and most flavorful dish imaginable. When I eat it, there is a burst of its essence and flavors on my palate.

1 pound linguine
Kosher salt
2 tablespoons unsalted butter
3 tablespoons extra virgin olive oil
2 small shallots, finely minced
2 tablespoons roughly torn fresh basil leaves
2 tablespoons fresh thyme leaves
2 tablespoons roughly torn fresh tarragon leaves
2 tablespoons roughly chopped fresh rosemary leaves
2 tablespoons roughly chopped fresh dill
1 pinch red pepper flakes
1 pinch freshly grated nutmeg
Freshly ground black pepper
Freshly grated Parmesan

Heat a 5- to 6-quart pot of water over high heat and bring to a boil. Add the linguine and 2 tablespoons salt and bring to a second boil. Stir vigorously for the first 45 seconds so the linguine will not stick. Cook the linguine until al dente according to the package directions.

While the pasta is cooking, heat a large skillet over medium heat; add the butter and oil. Add the shallots and cook until the shallots are translucent, 2 to 3 minutes. Stir in the basil, thyme, tarragon, rosemary, dill, red pepper flakes, and nutmeg. Season with salt and pepper. Cook until the herbs are fragrant and almost crispy, another 2 minutes.

When the linguine is ready, reserve ½ cup pasta water. Drain the linguine and transfer it to the skillet with the sauce; toss well to coat. Drizzle some pasta water in if the sauce is too dry. Top with the Parmesan.

Pasta with Fennel and Almonds

Serves 4 to 6

I don't remember when my family started making this pasta, although I know it's a Sicilian pasta sauce that is traditionally made with a few anchovies melted into it. Since I am not a fan of anchovies, I have always made it without. If you like anchovies, by all means add them to this recipe after the fennel is cooked. This pasta has a wonderful contrast of the brightness of the fresh fennel and the crunchiness of the toasted almonds.

1 pound linguine
Kosher salt
1 large sweet onion, minced
4 tablespoons extra virgin olive oil
1 fennel bulb, trimmed, finely diced
2 anchovies in oil, drained (optional)
2 tablespoons minced fennel greens
¼ to ½ teaspoon red pepper flakes
Freshly ground black pepper
¾ cup chopped blanched almonds, lightly toasted
½ cup grated Parmesan

Heat a 5- to 6-quart pot of water over high heat and bring to a boil. Add the linguine and 2 tablespoons salt and bring to a second boil. Stir vigorously for the first 45 seconds so the linguine will not stick. Cook the linguine until al dente according to the package directions.

Heat a large skillet over medium heat. Add the onions and sauté without oil until the liquid from the onions has reduced, 3 to 4 minutes. Add 3 tablespoons oil and continue to sauté the onions until golden, 6 to 8 minutes. Add the remaining 1 tablespoon oil, then the fennel and cook until tender, 6 to 8 minutes. Add the anchovies, if using, and stir to break them up. Add the fennel greens, and red pepper flakes. Season with salt and pepper. Sauté another minute. At this point the sauce is ready. Taste for seasoning and adjust if needed.

In a small dry pan, toast the almonds over medium-low heat until just golden and fragrant, a few minutes, stirring often to prevent burning. Set aside to cool. Grind the almonds in a small food processor until finely chopped. If you grind them too much, you will have almond butter.

When the linguine is ready, drain it, and transfer it to the skillet with the sauce. Toss well to coat the linguine. Top with the warm toasted almonds and the Parmesan.

PASTA WITH ZUCCHINI AND MINT

Serves 4 to 6

As I write this recipe, I am warming up some leftover pasta with zucchini and mint that I made for unexpected company last night. This is one of my favorite summertime pasta dishes because the freshness of the mint marries beautifully with the zucchini. I have zucchini and mint already growing in my garden, and the rest of the ingredients are all in my pantry. This dish could also be made with basil and a little rosemary; I prefer the mint.

1 pound spaghetti or linguine
Kosher salt
½ large sweet onion, shredded on the large side of a box grater
3 to 4 tablespoons extra virgin olive oil, plus more for drizzling
3 cloves garlic, minced
4 medium zucchini, thinly sliced
Freshly ground black pepper
3 tablespoons roughly torn fresh mint leaves
½ cup freshly grated Parmesan or pecorino

Heat a 5- to 6-quart pot of water over high heat and bring to a boil. Add the spaghetti and 2 tablespoons salt and bring to a second boil. Stir vigorously for the first 45 seconds so the spaghetti will not stick. Cook the spaghetti until al dente according to the package directions.

While the pasta is cooking, heat a large skillet over medium heat. Add the onions and sauté without oil until the liquid from the onions has reduced, 3 to 4 minutes. Add 3 tablespoons oil and continue to sauté the onions until golden, 6 to 8 minutes. Add the garlic and cook about 1 minute. Raise the heat to medium-high. Add the zucchini and cook, stirring occasionally, until the zucchini is golden but not mushy, 8 to 10 minutes. Season with salt and pepper. If the sauce is too dry, add the remaining 1 tablespoon oil. Add the mint, remove from heat, and stir well.

When the spaghetti is ready, drain it, and transfer it to the skillet with the sauce. Toss well to coat. Serve hot, topped with the Parmesan and a drizzle of extra virgin olive oil.

PASTA WITH RICOTTA AND DILL PESTO

Serves 4 to 6

I immediately fell in love with this pasta sauce when I first made it. When I was young, we ate pasta with ricotta often when it was too hot to cook. Later in life, I discovered my love for dill. This dish combines the fresh taste of the dill and the sweetness of the ricotta. A great advantage to this sauce is that by the time the pasta is cooked, the sauce is ready because it does not require any cooking.

1 pound tagliatelle or fettuccini
Kosher salt
1 bunch fresh dill, leaves and about 2 inches of the stems
2 cloves garlic, roughly chopped
⅓ cup pine nuts, lightly toasted
⅓ cup grated Parmesan, plus more for serving
Freshly ground black pepper
¼ cup or more extra virgin olive oil
8 ounces fresh ricotta, at room temperature

Heat a 5- to 6-quart pot of water over high heat and bring to a boil. Add the pasta and 2 tablespoons salt and bring to a second boil. Stir vigorously for the first 45 seconds so the pasta will not stick. Cook the pasta until al dente according to the package directions.

While the pasta cooks, place the dill, garlic, pine nuts, and Parmesan in a food processor. Season with salt and pepper. Pulse a few times to finely chop. With the motor running, drizzle in the olive oil a little at a time, until you achieve a creamy consistency, then transfer to a small bowl.

Place the ricotta in a large bowl and beat by hand with a wooden spoon for about a minute. Add the dill pesto and mix until the ricotta and the pesto are well combined.

When the pasta is ready, drain it, and transfer it to a serving bowl. Add the ricotta mixture, and fold to mix well. Top with extra grated Parmesan and black pepper.

Tip: *I always beat my ricotta before using it in any recipe. The ricotta has been packed in its container for a while, and sometimes it can be a little dense and gritty. Beating or mixing it first brings it back to a creamy consistency.*

PASTA WITH SAUSAGE AND CAULIFLOWER

Serves 4 to 6

When my husband and I met, he couldn't believe the numerous variations of pasta sauces available. I told him that Pasta with Sausage and Cauliflower was one of the most popular Sicilian dishes. Because sausage was inexpensive, we came up with many ways to cook it. Despite the unusual pairing of the two main ingredients, it is a delicious combination. Italians love vegetables so much that we have them at every meal, and many times vegetables are ingredients in our pasta sauces. This sauce is traditionally paired with orecchiette (little ears) pasta. It didn't take long before my husband was hooked on this pasta dish! How do you win a man's heart?

1 medium head cauliflower, cut into florets
1 pound orecchiette
Kosher salt
2 to 3 tablespoons extra virgin olive oil, divided
3 cloves garlic, minced
1 pound ground Italian sausage (mild, hot, or mixed)
1½ cups dry white wine
1½ cups chicken or vegetable broth
Freshly ground black pepper
1 pinch red pepper flakes
½ pound sharp provolone, cut in small cubes
⅓ cup grated Parmesan, plus more for serving
2 tablespoons roughly chopped fresh Italian parsley leaves for garnish

Heat a 5- to 6-quart pot of water over high heat; add the cauliflower and bring it to a boil. Cook until al dente, 10 to 15 minutes. Scoop out the cauliflower; keep the water boiling. Set the cauliflower aside.

Add the orecchiette and 2 tablespoons salt to the boiling water. Bring to a second boil. Stir vigorously for the first 45 seconds so the orecchiette will not stick. Cook the orecchiette until al dente according to the package directions.

While the pasta cooks, heat a large skillet over medium heat. Add 2 tablespoons oil and the garlic and sauté until the garlic is just golden, about 1 minute. Add the remaining 1 tablespoon oil and the sausage and sauté until cooked through and browned. Add the wine and reduce for about 2 minutes. Add the cauliflower and broth. Season with salt and pepper and stir in the red pepper flakes. Cook an additional 8 to 10 minutes.

When the orecchiette is ready, reserve ½ cup of the hot pasta water. Drain the orecchiette and transfer it to the skillet with the sauce. Reduce the heat to low, stir in the provolone and Parmesan. Cook until the cheeses have just melted. If the orecchiette is too dry, stir in the reserved pasta water. Transfer to individual bowls, and top with parsley and grated Parmesan. Serve hot.

Pasta with Tomatoes and Golden Bread Crumbs

Serves 4 to 6

Pasta first courses are a main event in an Italian household. When friends or relatives come over, I want to make a pasta dish that they will cherish, something simple and traditional we can enjoy together. When it comes to food and entertaining, I say the simpler the better. This is a simple unpretentious dish that I top with hot toasted bread crumbs and cheese. It's one I've made often for my kids. Topping pasta or vegetables dishes with toasted bread crumbs is very common in Southern Italian cooking.

FOR THE PASTA:
1 pound thin linguine
Kosher salt

FOR THE SAUCE:
3 to 4 tablespoons extra virgin olive oil
4 cloves garlic, thinly sliced
2 pints grape or cherry tomatoes, halved
2 to 3 tablespoons torn fresh basil leaves
Kosher salt
Freshly ground black pepper

FOR THE TOPPING:
1 ½ cups fresh Italian bread crumbs
½ cup freshly shaved Parmesan
Freshly ground black pepper
2 tablespoons extra virgin olive oil

FOR THE ASSEMBLY:
2 tablespoons finely torn fresh basil leaves

To make the pasta:
Heat a 5- to 6-quart pot of water over high heat and bring to a boil. Add the linguine and 2 tablespoons salt and bring to a second boil. Stir vigorously for the first 45 seconds so the linguine will not stick. Cook the linguine until al dente according to the package directions.

To make the sauce:

Heat a large skillet over medium heat. Add the oil and garlic and sauté until the garlic is barely golden, about 1 minute. Add the tomatoes and cook, tossing occasionally, until they are soft but still hold their shape, 5 to 6 minutes. Add the basil, and season with salt and pepper.

To make the topping:

Combine the bread crumbs, Parmesan, and some pepper in a small bowl. Mix everything together well with your fingertips or a spoon. Heat oil in a sauté pan over low heat. Add the breadcrumb mixture to the pan, and cook, stirring frequently, until the mixture is toasted and golden. Remove from the heat and set aside.

Assembly:

When the linguine is ready, drain it, and transfer it to the skillet with the sauce, toss well to coat. Transfer to bowls, top with the breadcrumb mixture and some basil.

PASTA WITH TUNA AND TOMATO SAUCE

Serves 4 to 6

I watched my grandfather and mother make this dish often. We had no kitchen tools other than a large fork and wooden spoons. Even though I now have measuring cups in my kitchen, I still use the empty tomato paste can to measure the water to use in this recipe. I count how many tomato-paste cans of water I use. It's an old method that still works for me and takes me back to the old traditions.

When the tuna is added to this sauce, it takes on the sweet taste of the tomato paste and the briny taste of the capers. This is yet another dish that I make because of the convenience of the ingredients from my pantry.

1 pound spaghetti or linguine
Kosher salt
1 medium sweet onion, minced
2 to 3 tablespoons extra virgin olive oil
2 cloves garlic, minced
1 (12-ounce) can tomato paste, reserve the empty can
2 teaspoons granulated sugar
1 bay leaf
20 capers in brine, drained
½ teaspoon freshly ground black pepper
2 (5-ounce) cans albacore tuna in water, well drained and flaked
2 to 3 tablespoons chopped fresh Italian parsley leaves

Heat a 5- to 6-quart pot of water over high heat and bring to a boil. Add the spaghetti and 2 tablespoons salt and bring to a second boil. Stir vigorously for the first 45 seconds so the spaghetti will not stick. Cook the spaghetti until al dente according to the package directions.

While the pasta is cooking, heat a large skillet over medium heat. Add the onions and sauté without oil until the liquid from the onions has reduced, 3 to 4 minutes. Add the oil and continue to sauté the onions until golden, 6 to 8 minutes. Add the garlic and cook about a minute. Push the onions and garlic to the sides of the pan. Add the tomato paste into the center of the pan and cook undisturbed for 2 minutes. (Leaving the tomato paste undisturbed helps to caramelize it which intensifies the flavor of the sauce.) Stir everything together. Cook for another 2 minutes undisturbed. Add the sugar, bay leaf, capers, pepper, and ½ teaspoon salt. Stir well, scraping the bottom of the pan. Add 2 tomato paste cans of water and mix well again. Bring to a boil over medium-high heat. Stir quickly, lower the heat to low, and simmer 6 to 8 minutes. Stir in the tuna; simmer for another 5 minutes. Remove and discard the bay leaf.

When the spaghetti is ready, drain it, and transfer it to the skillet with the sauce and toss well to coat. Serve hot topped with the parsley.

BAKED PASTA
(PASTA AL FORNO)

Neapolitan Lasagna with Mini Meatballs

Serves 4 to 6

In Southern Italy, lasagna is made with red sauce and ricotta, but some of the other ingredients can vary. Sometimes, hard-cooked eggs are added, sometimes a meat sauce or sausage is used. In this recipe, I make the lasagna with small meatballs. Whatever ingredients are used, the process of making it doesn't change. Make sure you have just enough sauce but be careful not to use so much that it overwhelms the dish. Make sure that you can taste all of the individual ingredients in the lasagna, that no one ingredient overpowers the pasta or the filling. You can make the meatballs ahead to make it easier to assemble.

Note: *Before starting to assemble the lasagna, have the meatballs, marinara sauce, and ricotta mixture ready for a fast and easy assembly. Start with making the meatballs and the sauce ahead. The ricotta mixture can be made while the pasta is cooking. As soon as the pasta is ready and drained, then you can begin assembly. All will fall into place.*

FOR THE MEATBALLS:
Oil for baking sheet
4 slices day-old French bread
¼ cup whole milk
2 pounds lean ground beef
2 tablespoons finely chopped fresh Italian parsley leaves
¼ cup finely minced red onion
6 cloves garlic, finely minced
½ cup grated pecorino
2 large eggs, beaten
1 cup dry Italian bread crumbs
Kosher salt
Freshly ground black pepper

FOR THE PASTA:
Kosher salt
1 pound lasagna noodles

FOR THE ASSEMBLY:
8 ounces whole milk ricotta
6 to 7 cups Basic Marinara Sauce (page 40)
1½ cups grated pecorino
3 to 4 tablespoons roughly torn fresh basil leaves, divided
Freshly ground black pepper

To make the meatballs:

Heat the oven to 400°F. Lightly coat a rimmed baking sheet with oil.

Soak the bread in the milk for a few minutes, squeeze out and discard the milk.

Combine bread, beef, parsley, onions, garlic, pecorino, eggs, and bread crumbs in a large mixing bowl. Season with salt and pepper. Mix well.

Form 1-inch meatballs without packing them down and place them on the prepared baking sheet. Arrange the meatballs on the baking sheet so they do not touch. Bake, uncovered, until the bottoms are browned, 5 to 6 minutes. Turn the meatballs over once, and bake until browned, 3 to 4 minutes.

To cook the lasagna noodles:

Heat a 5- to 6-quart pot of water over high heat and bring to a boil. Add the lasagna noodles and 2 tablespoons salt and bring to a second boil. Stir vigorously for the first 45 seconds so the lasagna noodles will not stick. Cook the lasagna noodles 2 minutes less than the package directions; they will continue to cook in the oven. When ready, drain the lasagna noodles gently so they don't tear, and spread them flat on baking sheets to cool.

To prepare the ricotta:

Place the ricotta in a small bowl and beat with a wooden spoon for a few minutes. Add 2 tablespoons marinara sauce and mix again.

Assembly:

Heat the oven to 350°F.

Spread a few tablespoons of the marinara sauce on the bottom of a 9- x 13-inch glass baking pan. Sprinkle some pecorino, basil, and pepper on top. Add one-third of the lasagna noodles in a layer to cover the sauce. Spread a few tablespoons of the ricotta mixture on top of the lasagna. The ricotta does not have to cover the entire surface. Arrange about one-third of the meatballs on top of ricotta. Spoon about one-fourth of marinara sauce on top of the meatballs. Sprinkle with one-third of the pecorino, basil, and pepper. Repeat this layering twice. Make sure you use about the same amount of ingredients for each layer. Top with the remaining marinara sauce. When finished, place the lasagna in the oven and bake until bubbling, about 30 minutes. When ready, remove from the oven and allow the lasagna to cool for 10 to 15 minutes before slicing. If you don't wait, the lasagna will not have time to firm up, and it will be a soupy mess when you cut it.

SICILIAN PASTA
AND EGGPLANT TIMBALLO
Serves 4 to 6

A timballo is an Italian casserole dish or the mold the casserole is cooked in. Food baked in a timballo has a crispy exterior, making it easy to unmold. Sicilian Pasta and Eggplant Timballo is a dish I prepare for Sunday dinners, birthdays or Christmas Eve—it is always a success! It is convenient to make because it can be prepared in advance and is easily transported. The eggplant used in this dish will keep the timballo together, because it encloses the pasta and keeps the filling inside. Once the timballo is slightly cooled and unmolded, it will be easy to cut into slices.

5 medium eggplants, sliced lengthwise ¼-inch thick
Extra virgin olive oil for brushing
Kosher salt
Freshly ground black pepper
1 pound mezze penne
6 cups Quick Meat Sauce, divided (page 41)
1¼ cups grated pecorino, divided
1 cup torn fresh basil leaves
3 large eggs, lightly beaten
1 cup frozen petite peas, thawed

Heat the oven to 400°F.

Using a pastry brush, generously brush the eggplant slices on both sides with oil and sprinkle with salt and pepper. Place on a baking sheet in a single layer. You may need to use two baking sheets to fit all the slices. If you use two sheets, bake them individually or the eggplant will steam instead of roast. Bake until the eggplant becomes slightly golden on both sides, turning only once, 15 to 18 minutes.

Heat a 5- to 6-quart pot of water over high heat and bring to a boil. Add the penne and 2 tablespoons salt; bring to a second boil. Stir vigorously for the first 45 seconds so the penne will not stick. Cook the penne 2 minutes less than the time on the package directions because the penne will continue to cook in the oven.

When the penne is ready, drain it, and transfer it to a large bowl. Fold in 2 cups meat sauce, ¼ cup pecorino, and the basil. Allow to cool 10 to 15 minutes, then fold in the eggs.

Assembling the timballo:

Line a 12-cup Bundt pan with the cooked eggplant slices, making sure that the slices overlap, with no gaps, and hang over the edge of the pan. Setting them on the diagonal makes an especially beautiful dish. You will probably have to place them first around the outer side and then make the next row around the post in the middle. Reserve a few slices to cover the top. Fill the pan with one third of the penne mixture, press down to make sure it is filling evenly, spread about one-third of the peas over the penne, dollop on a few tablespoons of sauce, top with ¼ cup pecorino. Repeat the layer two more times, pressing down on the penne each time. You want to build a sturdy structure.

Fold the eggplant slices up over the top of the penne to cover. Add the remaining slices of cooked eggplant on top to enclose the timballo. Bake the timballo until a knife inserted comes out clean and it feels as if the filling is not loose, about 30 minutes. Remove from the oven and allow to rest 10 to 15 minutes.

Place a large plate over the Bundt pan. Gently invert the Bundt pan to release the timballo onto the plate. Cut in wedges, sprinkle with the remaining ¼ cup pecorino, and serve with warmed remaining meat sauce on the side.

Note: *To make ahead you can either assemble the timballo and refrigerate it until ready to bake; or bake it and then refrigerate still in the bundt pan and reheat when ready to serve.*

Couscous are dry pellets, typically made of durum wheat flour. Much like pasta in Italy, couscous is prepared in many variations in the Maghreb. The versions differ from country to country among the villages, and even from one family to another, depending on the availability of ingredients. Couscous is often made with lamb, chicken, mutton, beef, fish, and vegetables. In Sicily, it is usually served with fish. Couscous is accompanied by a mixture of the broth it is cooked and dressed in and a spicy sauce called harissa, which is served on the side, so that each person can add it as desired.

It has been, and still is in some countries, a tradition in Maghreb for a large group of people to sit together to eat couscous from a large round dish in the middle of the table. Some people still eat their couscous by forming it into a ball around a piece of a vegetable, meat, or fish. Others, like in our Italian home, place the couscous in individual deep serving plates and add the vegetables, meat, or fish with a little broth on top.

Making the couscous from scratch is a labor-intensive process that usually is done a few times a year by family and friends who come together to make the couscous by hand and then take their portions home. If you do not have the time or skill to follow the traditional process, you can use the couscous that is easily found in supermarkets. That couscous is usually steamed pasta that has been dried. The instructions on the package say to simply add some boiling water to make it ready for consumption. My grandfather taught me a step that I add to my couscous making. I place the dry couscous in a bowl, drizzle on a little olive oil, and rub the couscous with my hands, making sure that the pellets are coated with the oil. I then season it with salt and pepper and run my hands through it one more time. Next, I pour in the hot water, quickly stir, and cover the couscous and let it sit undisturbed for 10 minutes. At the end of 10 minutes, I fluff the couscous with a fork. It does not stick, and it is much more flavorful.

Flavors of the Maghreb and Southern Italy

SEFFA COUSCOUS FOR FESTIVE OCCASIONS

Serves 4 to 6

In the Maghreb, sometimes couscous is served at the end of the meal as a delicacy called "*seffa*," which is made with dried fruit, almonds, cinnamon, and sugar. It is traditional to serve *seffa* with milk flavored with orange blossom water as a dessert or with milk whey as a light soup for dinner. This North African dish is customarily served in large mounds during festive gatherings such as weddings and anniversaries. And when a guest comes to your home, *seffa* is offered as a symbol of generosity, friendliness, and warmth.

3 cups dry couscous
1½ tablespoons extra virgin olive oil
1 teaspoon kosher salt
Freshly ground black pepper
3 cups boiling water
2 teaspoons rosewater
4 tablespoons (½ stick) unsalted butter, melted and warm
¾ cup golden raisins
½ cup pitted dried apricots, whole or sliced
½ cup pitted dates, whole or sliced
½ cup slivered almonds, lightly toasted
2 teaspoons ground cinnamon
Brown sugar to serve

Place the dry couscous in a large bowl and drizzle the oil on top. Rub the couscous between your hands to coat the couscous with oil. You will know that the couscous is well coated if some pellets stick to your hands. Add the salt, and season with pepper. Run your hands through it one more time to mix well. Pour in the boiling water and rosewater; quickly stir with a wooden spoon. Cover the couscous with a plate and let it sit, undisturbed, for at least 10 minutes.

Once the couscous is ready, remove the plate, and use a fork to break up and loosen the couscous. Add the melted butter and stir with a wooden spoon until well blended. Gently fold in the raisins, apricots, and dates. Transfer the couscous to a festive platter and create a mound in the shape of a cone. Scatter the toasted almonds around the base of the mound. Sprinkle cinnamon around the mound creating either a stripe or dot pattern.

Serve at room temperature with a small bowl of light brown sugar on the side for your guests to sprinkle on top.

COUSCOUS WITH LAMB AND VEGETABLES
Serves 4 to 6

Couscous with Lamb and Vegetables is one of the most popular ethnic dishes of Maghrebi cuisine. For us, the Italians, this was a recipe we typically served during an Easter meal because eating lamb for Easter was customary in the Catholic culture. For other Mediterranean countries, this dish could be enjoyed anytime of the year. Tunisians serve fresh buttermilk and olives along with this dish.

FOR THE LAMB AND VEGETABLES:
4 tablespoons extra virgin olive oil
2 pounds shoulder or leg of lamb, cut in 1-inch cubes, patted dry with paper towels
2 large onions, diced
2 tablespoons tomato paste
2 teaspoons Harissa (page 188)
4 cloves garlic, minced
2 small bell peppers, seeds and ribs removed, diced
2 turnips, peeled and diced
4 carrots, peeled and diced
3 large Yukon gold potatoes, peeled and diced
1 teaspoon ground cumin
½ teaspoon ground coriander
½ teaspoon Ras el Hanout Spice Blend (page 189)
Kosher salt
Freshly ground black pepper

FOR THE COUSCOUS:
3 cups dry couscous
1 tablespoon extra virgin olive oil
½ teaspoon kosher salt
Freshly ground black pepper
3 cups boiling water

FOR SERVING:
3 tablespoons chopped fresh Italian parsley leaves

To make the lamb and vegetables:

Heat the oil in a 5- to 6-quart pot over medium heat. Add the lamb in two batches, and brown on all sides, 10 to 12 minutes for each batch. As each batch is browned, transfer the lamb to a plate and set aside.

Add the onions to the pan, and cook until soft and golden, 6 to 8 minutes. Add the tomato paste and Harissa; cook for 5 minutes, stirring continually. Add the garlic, bell peppers, turnips, carrots, and potatoes, mixing well. Cook, stirring often, until the vegetables are just golden, 6 to 8 minutes. Add the cumin, coriander, and Ras el Hanout. Season with salt and pepper; stir about 1 minute. Return the lamb to the pot. Add enough water to the pan to cover the vegetables and lamb by about 3 inches; stir well. Bring to a boil, cover, reduce heat, and simmer until the lamb is fully cooked and tender, 1 to 1½ hours.

To make the couscous:

Place the dry couscous in a large bowl, and drizzle 1 tablespoon oil on top. Rub the couscous between your hands to coat the couscous with oil. You will know that the couscous is well coated if some pellets stick to your hands. Add the salt, and season with pepper. Run your hands through it one more time to mix well. Pour in the boiling water; quickly stir with a wooden spoon. Cover the couscous with a plate and let it sit, undisturbed, for at least 10 minutes. Once the couscous is ready, remove the plate, and use a fork to break up and loosen the couscous.

To serve:

Serve 1 cup of couscous in a bowl, and ladle some of the lamb and vegetable stew on top. Garnish with the chopped parsley.

FRIDAY'S COUSCOUS

Serves 4 to 6

Friday's Couscous developed because of the Catholic tradition that we observed of eating fish on Fridays. Respecting the religious rituals in those days was a way of life. Friday was always a special day for enjoying fish or seafood. Be selective when you choose the fish for this dish: choose the freshest and highest quality fish for a tastier couscous.

FOR THE VEGETABLES AND FISH:
2 tablespoons extra virgin olive oil
1 large red onion, minced
2 carrots, peeled and in small dice
2 zucchini, in small dice
2 turnips, in small dice
2 ripe tomatoes, in small dice
1 stalk celery, minced
2 tablespoons tomato paste
4 cups vegetable, fish, or chicken broth
1 pinch saffron
1 teaspoon ground cumin
1 teaspoon ground coriander
1 pinch red pepper flakes
Kosher salt
Freshly ground black pepper
1 pound fish (haddock, cod, or pollack), skin removed, cut into 2-inch strips, patted dry with paper towels
1 cup canned chickpeas, drained

FOR THE COUSCOUS:
3 cups dry couscous
1 tablespoon extra virgin olive oil
Kosher salt
Freshly ground black pepper
3 cups boiling water

FOR SERVING:
1 lemon
Fresh Italian parsley leaves, roughly chopped, for garnish
Harissa (page 188)

To make the vegetables and fish:

Heat the oil in a large saucepan over medium heat. Add the onions, carrots, zucchini, turnips, tomatoes, and celery; sauté until mostly golden, 5 to 8 minutes. Add the tomato paste and sauté for 1 minute. Add the broth, saffron, cumin, coriander, and red pepper flakes. Season with salt and pepper. Stir well and bring to a boil. Reduce heat to low, and simmer until vegetables are soft, 10 to 12 minutes. Add the fish and chickpeas. Let cook until the fish is cooked through, 5 to 6 minutes. Taste the stew for seasoning, adjust if needed.

To make the couscous:

Place the dry couscous in a bowl, and drizzle the oil on top. Rub the couscous between your hands to coat the couscous with oil. You will know that the couscous is well coated if some pellets stick to your hands. Add the salt, and season with pepper. Run your hands through it one more time to mix well. Pour in the boiling water; quickly stir with a wooden spoon. Cover the couscous with a plate, and let it sit, undisturbed, for at least 10 minutes. Once the couscous is ready, remove the plate, and use a fork to break up and loosen the couscous.

To serve:

Serve a scoop of couscous topped with some fish and vegetable stew in each bowl. Squeeze fresh lemon juice over the stew and top with fresh parsley. Serve Harissa on the side.

RICE with LENTILS and CARAMELIZED ONIONS

Serves 4 to 6

My grandfather would make a huge amount of this rice and lentils dish when we had a big family gathering. He never put the fried onions on top for such a large group. Traditionally, this dish is made with crispy fried onions. I like putting my own perspective on this recipe, so once the onions are cooked, I add a drizzle of thick balsamic vinegar and cook it for a couple minutes. This gives the onions an *agrodolce* (sweet and sour) taste that combines well with the cooked rice and lentils.

FOR THE RICE AND LENTILS:
2 tablespoons extra virgin olive oil
1 large sweet onion, minced
1 teaspoon ground coriander
½ teaspoon ground cumin
3 ½ cups chicken or vegetable broth
1 cup brown lentils
1 cup jasmine or long-grain rice
Kosher salt
Freshly ground black pepper

FOR THE BALSAMIC ONION TOPPING:
3 tablespoons extra virgin olive oil
2 large sweet onions, thinly sliced
Kosher salt
Freshly ground black pepper
4 tablespoons aged balsamic vinegar

FOR SERVING:
2 to 3 tablespoons roughly chopped fresh cilantro
2 scallions, green part only, chopped

To make the rice and lentils:

In a large frying pan, heat the olive oil. Add the minced onions. Sauté over medium heat until soft and golden, 10 to 15 minutes. Stir in the coriander and cumin and cook until fragrant, about 30 seconds. Set aside to mix with rice and lentils.

Place the broth and lentils in a 4-quart pot with a lid. Bring to a boil, reduce the heat to a simmer and cover. Simmer for 15 minutes. Stir in the sautéed onions and the rice. Season with salt and pepper. Simmer, covered, until the rice and lentils are soft, another 20 to 25 minutes.

To make the balsamic and onion topping:

While the rice is cooking, wipe the oil out of the frying pan with paper towels. Add the oil for the topping to the frying pan and heat it over medium heat. Add the sliced onions, and cook, stirring, until soft and browned, 15 to 20 minutes. Season with salt and pepper. Add the balsamic vinegar, and let it cook, stirring occasionally, until slightly thickened, for about 2 minutes. The onion slices will take on a caramel color.

To serve:

Place the rice and lentil mixture in a bowl or on a platter. Top with the balsamic onions, cilantro, and scallion greens.

SAFFRON COUSCOUS WITH PEAS, RAISINS, AND ALMONDS

Serves 4 to 6

In the Mediterranean region, saffron is known as the spice of good mood. It is said that, because of its color and scent, saffron brings cheerfulness to the table. Couscous with the sweet peas and raisins is exceptionally fragrant. This is a dish that can be served with any fish or meat entrée. It can also be a hearty vegetarian entrée.

2 cups dry couscous
2 tablespoons extra virgin olive oil, divided
Kosher salt
Freshly ground black pepper
2 ½ cups vegetable broth
¼ teaspoon saffron threads
1 cup frozen peas, thawed
½ cup slivered almonds
½ cup golden raisins

Place the dry couscous in a large bowl. Drizzle 1 tablespoon oil on top. Rub the couscous between your hands to coat the couscous with oil. You will know that the couscous is well coated if some pellets stick to your hands. Season with salt and pepper. Run your hands through it one more time to mix well.

Place the broth and saffron in a small saucepan; bring it to a boil. As soon as the broth comes to a boil, pour it into the couscous; stir quickly with a wooden spoon. Cover with a plate, and let sit, undisturbed, for least 10 minutes. Once the couscous is ready, remove the plate and use a fork to break up and loosen the couscous. Stir in the peas and remaining 1 tablespoon olive oil.

Toast the almonds in a small dry skillet over low heat, shaking the pan often. Watch carefully so they don't burn. Remove from the heat and add the raisins. Add the almonds and raisins to the couscous and mix again. Taste, and adjust seasoning if necessary. Serve warm or at room temperature.

Flavors of the Maghreb and Southern Italy

Spicy Tunisian Chicken Couscous

Serves 4 to 6

I make this couscous with a whole chicken that I cut into smaller pieces. If you want to skip this step, you can always purchase a cut-up chicken, or use eight bone-in chicken thighs to simplify the recipe. The unmistakable perfume from its spices and the piquancy of the Harissa give this couscous a unique taste.

FOR THE CHICKEN:
3 tablespoons extra virgin olive oil
1 (4-pound) chicken, cut in eighths, patted dry with paper towels
1 large onion, diced
1½ teaspoons ground cumin
1½ teaspoons ground cinnamon
1½ teaspoons paprika
½ teaspoon ground cayenne
½ teaspoon Ras el Hanout Spice Blend (page 189)
Kosher salt
4 cloves garlic, minced
3 ounces tomato paste
2 cups chicken or vegetable broth, plus more if needed
2 carrots, peeled and cut in small cubes
4 cups cubed peeled fresh pumpkin
2 tablespoons Harissa (page 188)
2 zucchini, cut in small cubes
1 (16-ounce) can chickpeas, drained

FOR THE COUSCOUS:
3 cups dry couscous
1 tablespoon extra virgin olive oil
Kosher salt
Freshly ground black pepper
3 cups boiling chicken or vegetable broth

To make the chicken:

In a Dutch oven or a 12-inch saucepan, heat the olive oil over medium-high heat. Cook the chicken in batches until golden on all sides. Transfer the chicken to a plate and set aside.

Add the onions, cumin, cinnamon, paprika, cayenne, and Ras el Hanout to the pot. Season with the salt. Stir and cook until the onions soften and the spices become fragrant, 3 to 4 minutes. Add the garlic, stir, and cook for about 30 seconds.

Add the tomato paste and 1 cup broth, deglazing the pan by stirring up all of the browned bits. Return the chicken to the pot. Add just enough broth to cover the chicken. Bring to a boil. Reduce the heat to a simmer, and cover. Cook about 30 minutes, stirring occasionally and adding more broth if the pan becomes too dry.

Stir in the carrots, pumpkin, and Harissa; cook 10 more minutes. Add the zucchini and chickpeas; mix well. Continue cooking until the zucchini and pumpkin are tender, about 10 more minutes.

To make the couscous:

Place the dry couscous in a bowl, and drizzle 1 tablespoon oil on top. Rub the couscous between your hands to coat the couscous with oil. You will know that it is well coated if some pellets stick to your hands. Season with salt and pepper. Run your hands through it one more time to mix well. Pour in the hot broth; quickly stir with a wooden spoon. Cover the couscous with a plate and let it sit, undisturbed, for at least 10 minutes. Once the couscous is ready, remove the plate, and use a fork to break up and loosen the couscous.

To serve:

Serve the couscous in individual bowls with some chicken stew ladled on top.

Tunisian Couscous Salad

Serves 4 to 6

This is a fresh and light salad my family brought on Sunday outings to the beach. We had no car, so we took a train. We filled a large picnic basket with Tunisian sandwiches, cold salads, and fresh fruit. This salad is easy to transport because it can be eaten at room temperature or cold. I serve it in the summer months when I have fresh vegetables in my garden—it always reminds me of our family ritual at the beach.

FOR THE COUSCOUS:
2 cups dry couscous
1½ tablespoons extra virgin olive oil
2 cups boiling water
½ teaspoon kosher salt

FOR THE DRESSING:
¼ cup olive oil
Juice of ½ to 1 lemon
1 large clove garlic, finely minced
1 to 1½ teaspoons ground cumin
½ teaspoon ground cayenne
⅓ red onion, minced
Kosher salt
Freshly ground black pepper

FOR THE SALAD:
½ yellow bell pepper, ribs and seeds removed, diced
½ orange bell pepper, ribs and seeds removed, diced
2 ripe Roma tomatoes, seeded and cut into ¼-inch dice
2 scallions, minced
½ English cucumber, peeled and cut into ¼-inch dice
½ cup cooked corn
2 to 3 tablespoons finely chopped fresh mint leaves
2 hard-cooked eggs, quartered
½ cup Moroccan or other black oil-cured olives, pitted

To make the couscous: Place the dry couscous in a large bowl and drizzle the oil on top. Rub the couscous between your hands to coat the couscous with oil. You will know that the couscous is well coated if some pellets stick to your hands. Pour the boiling water over the couscous. Add the salt and quickly stir. Cover with a plate and let stand for 10 to 15 minutes undisturbed.

To make the dressing: In a large bowl, combine the olive oil, lemon juice, garlic, cumin, cayenne pepper, and red onion. Season with salt and pepper; whisk together well.

To make the salad: Add the peppers, tomatoes, scallions, cucumbers, and corn to the dressing; toss well to coat. Taste for seasoning and adjust to taste. When the couscous is ready, fluff it with a fork. Add the dressing with the vegetables; toss to combine. Add the fresh mint and mix again. Serve with the hard-cooked eggs and black olives on top.

CHICKEN

Today, in many cultures, chicken is very present in most kitchens all year long. From soup to countless roasted, baked, stewed, and fried dishes, chicken is a versatile ingredient. When I was growing up, we had no ovens. All the dishes were made in a pot on the stove. Sometimes I think that a stovetop method is the best for creating more flavorful dishes. But I know baking and roasting have become the easiest methods of cooking for today's busy household.

Chickens didn't always come already cut up and packaged. We cut up our own chicken to suit the dish we wanted to create. Thighs or legs were always browned and then braised in broth or wine for a long time. Breasts were flattened to create several Italian or Maghrebi dishes. Any leftovers would be boiled with the bones to create a chicken stock to make soups or to add to other chicken dishes. Every part of the chicken was eaten up; only the bones were left behind.

In this section, please enjoy classic chicken recipes made with fresh lemons, herbs, vegetables, spices, wine, and other ingredients, both exotic and simple. Discover new recipes that will become your favorites to serve to your family, friends, and guests.

AROMATIC CHICKEN AND DRIED FRUIT TAGINE

Serves 4 to 6

Tagines are popular traditional Berber dishes in Maghrebi cuisine. Tagines are composed of stewed meat, usually chicken or lamb, with tomatoes, almonds, plums, and some mild but fragrant spices. On my first visit back to Tunisia, my aunt prepared this dish for me upon my arrival. I relished watching her as she cooked it in the clay pot, which is also called a tagine. It was an exceptional evening to remember.

10 pitted prunes, halved
18 to 20 pitted dried apricots
¾ cup golden raisins
Warm water for soaking the fruit
4 chicken thighs and 4 chicken legs with skin on, patted dry with paper towels
Kosher salt
Freshly ground black pepper
2 to 3 tablespoons extra virgin olive oil
2 tablespoons unsalted butter
1 large sweet onion, diced
4 to 5 cloves garlic, minced
1 pinch red pepper flakes
4 ripe Roma tomatoes, diced
2 medium zucchini, diced
1 cup whole blanched almonds
2 tablespoons Ras el Hanout Spice Blend (page 189)
2 sticks cinnamon
1 tablespoon ground turmeric
4 cups warm chicken broth or warm water
4 tablespoons honey
3 to 4 tablespoons chopped fresh cilantro

Place the prunes, apricots, and raisins in warm water to cover. Let sit to soften for about 15 minutes. Drain, and set aside.

Season the chicken with salt and pepper. Add the oil and butter to a large heavy-bottomed pan over medium-high heat. Add the chicken pieces and sauté until golden on all sides. Do not crowd the pan; you may need to cook them in batches. Transfer to a plate, cover with aluminum foil, and reserve.

Flavors of the Maghreb and Southern Italy

Using the same pan, reduce the heat to medium-low, add the onions, and cook until softened, 5 to 8 minutes. Add the garlic, red pepper flakes, and tomatoes; cook for 5 minutes. Add the zucchini, almonds, dried fruits, Ras el Hanout, cinnamon sticks, and turmeric, and cook 2 to 3 minutes.

Return the chicken to the pan. Add the broth; bring to a boil. Reduce the heat to low and simmer, covered, stirring occasionally, until the chicken is cooked through, 30 to 35 minutes. Taste for seasoning and adjust as needed.

When the chicken is fully cooked, stir in the honey and cilantro. Remove and discard the cinnamon sticks. Serve warm with a side of couscous, pasta, potatoes, or rice.

CHICKEN AND SWEET POTATO TAGINE

Serves 4 to 6

Preparing Maghrebi cuisine is an art, especially when it comes to cooking tagines. It takes a little perseverance and patience to take simple ingredients and turn them into a savory, sweet, satisfying comfort dish like this one. This preparation offers another dimension of flavor to chicken and sweet potatoes.

8 chicken thighs or legs with skin on, patted dry with paper towels
Kosher salt
Freshly ground black pepper
3 tablespoons extra virgin olive oil
2 large onions, minced
3 large sweet potatoes, peeled and cut into ½-inch rounds
1 tablespoon ground cumin
1 tablespoon ground coriander
1 tablespoon ground ginger
1 teaspoon ground paprika
1 pinch red pepper flakes
¾ cup golden raisins, soaked in warm water and drained
4 cups warm chicken broth or warm water
2 to 3 tablespoons chopped fresh cilantro leaves
1 loaf crusty bread

Season the chicken with salt and pepper.

In a large heavy-bottomed pan, heat the oil over medium-low heat. When the oil is hot, add the onions and cook until softened, 8 to 10 minutes. Transfer the onions to a large bowl and set aside.

Increase the heat to medium, add the chicken and cook until golden on both sides, 15 to 20 minutes. Transfer the chicken to the bowl with the onions and set aside.

Add the sweet potatoes, cumin, coriander, ginger, paprika, red pepper flakes to the pan and cook, stirring often, for 2 to 3 minutes. Return the chicken and onions to the pan.

Add the raisins and broth. Bring to a boil, still over medium heat. Reduce heat to low, cover, and continue to cook, stirring occasionally, until the chicken is cooked through and the potatoes are tender, 30 to 35 minutes. When ready, add cilantro, and serve with a crusty bread to sop up all of the tasty juices.

CHICKEN, LEMON, AND HONEY BUNDLES

Serves 4 to 6

This is a dish I love to make whenever I have friends with children coming to dinner. Not only is it quick to prepare, but the chicken has a tangy lemon flavor with a slightly crispy sweet crust from the honey. It's perfect for an evening with friends. To make it even more special, I make the kids their own little individual bundles.

4 tablespoons honey
Zest and juice of ½ lemon
½ teaspoon paprika
½ teaspoon ground coriander
3 skinless, boneless chicken breast halves, cut into 1½-inch strips,
   patted dry with paper towels
Kosher salt
Freshly ground black pepper
Light olive oil for brushing
2 tablespoons minced fresh cilantro or parsley leaves

Heat the oven to 400°F. Cut four (8- x 6-inch) rectangles of parchment paper.

Place the honey, lemon zest and juice, paprika, and coriander in a bowl; whisk together well. Season the chicken with salt and pepper and add to the honey mixture. Mix well, making sure the chicken pieces are well coated. Cover with plastic wrap and refrigerate for about an hour.

Fold each piece of parchment paper in half; open them and brush the inside lightly with oil. Place one-quarter of the chicken pieces in the center of one half of each rectangle and divide any remaining honey mixture among the four bundles. Fold the parchment in half over the chicken. Starting at the folded edge, make small tight overlapping triangular folds around the outside edge, working your way around the parchment and forming a half moon. The parchment will look as though it had been crimped. When you reach the end, fold the last triangle over and tuck it into the preceding triangle to seal. Place the bundles on a rimmed baking sheet. Using your fingers, flick a few drops of water onto the bundles to prevent burning.

Bake for 15 minutes. The chicken should be cooked through; open one bundle to check. If it is ready, remove all of the bundles from the oven. If it's not ready, cook a few more minutes. Remove from the oven, and carefully open each bundle. Sprinkle the cilantro on top of the chicken. Transfer the bundles to dinner plates.

CHICKEN POLPETTINE

Serves 4 to 6

"*P*olpettine" is Italian for small meatballs. It's a dish we cooked up with leftover chicken meat boiled in broth that was made from chicken bouillon cubes. When we didn't have enough chicken, we mixed in lots of bread crumbs. I have modernized this recipe for today's cooks.

1 pound ground chicken or turkey
1 to 2 cups dry Italian bread crumbs
¾ cup grated Parmesan
2 or 3 large eggs
3 tablespoons finely minced fresh Italian parsley leaves
Kosher salt
Freshly ground black pepper
2 to 3 tablespoons extra virgin olive oil
2 large cloves garlic, minced
1 pinch red pepper flakes
1 cup dry white wine
2 cups chicken or vegetable broth
3 to 4 tablespoons chiffonade of fresh basil leaves

Combine the chicken, 1 cup bread crumbs, the Parmesan, 2 eggs, and the parsley in a large bowl. Season with salt and pepper and mix well. Take about a tablespoon of the chicken mixture and form a ball 1 to 1½-inches in diameter. The ball should be slightly firm and should hold its shape. If the *polpettine* are too dry to hold together, add another egg. If they are too wet, add more bread crumbs. Continue making the *polpettine* until you have used up all the chicken mixture. As you form the *polpettine*, place them on a platter or rimmed baking sheet.

In a large skillet over medium-low heat, add the oil, garlic, and red pepper flakes. Sauté for about 1 minute until the garlic is fragrant and barely golden. Add the wine and cook about 1 minute. Stir in the broth. Increase heat to medium and bring to a boil. Add the *polpettine*. Reduce heat to medium-low, cover the skillet, and simmer until the *polpettine* are cooked through, 10 to 15 minutes. As soon as the *polpettine* are ready, add the fresh basil on top and serve.

CHICKEN WITH CABBAGE AND GREEN OLIVES TAGINE

Serves 4 to 6

A tagine is a clay pot; the dishes made in the clay pot are also called "tagines." Those dishes are Maghrebi specialties that are made with different ingredients depending on the traditions of the families and the regions they come from. Each type of tagine is a family-friendly dish with its own special accent. These tagines are easy to make and are loved by all. Don't be intimidated by the long list of ingredients in tagine recipes; usually most of the ingredients are spices.

The traditional method of cooking with a tagine is to place it over coals. If you don't have coals available, cook it on the stovetop, not in the oven.

1 teaspoon ground coriander
1 teaspoon ground turmeric
1 teaspoon ground cumin
½ teaspoon ground cinnamon
8 chicken thighs or legs, with skin and bones, patted dry with paper towels
Kosher salt
Freshly ground black pepper
2 tablespoons extra virgin olive oil
2 sweet onions, minced
1 large ripe tomato, minced
1 medium head cabbage, hard core removed, shredded
2 cups hot water or hot broth, or more if needed
25 pitted green olives
2 to 3 tablespoons chopped fresh Italian parsley leaves

Mix the coriander, turmeric, cumin, and cinnamon together in a small bowl. Set aside.

Season the chicken pieces on both sides with salt and pepper.

Heat the oil in a large deep heavy-bottomed skillet over medium-high heat. Add the onions, tomatoes, and chicken. Cook, turning occasionally, until the chicken is golden brown on all sides, about 15 minutes.

Add the cabbage, broth, and spice mixture. Bring to a boil, then reduce heat to low. Cover, and cook until the cabbage is tender and the chicken is done, about 45 minutes. Check periodically for liquid; if the pot is dry, add some more hot broth. Add the olives and warm through. Taste for seasoning, adjust if needed. Transfer to a serving platter, sprinkle with parsley, and serve warm.

Maghrebi Chicken Brochettes

Serves 4 to 8

Ah, the perfume of these brochettes cooking in the streets! What pleasure and emotion this dish brings back with memories of Sunday strolls in downtown Tunis. Lining the avenues were street vendors selling lots of delicious foods including these mouth-watering brochettes.

Note: *It is best to marinate the chicken for these brochettes overnight. If you are using wooden skewers, you must soak them in warm water for at least 1 hour.*

4 skinless, boneless chicken breast halves, cut into 1½-inch cubes,
   patted dry with paper towels
Kosher salt
Freshly ground black pepper
12 ounces plain whole milk yogurt
2 tablespoons finely minced shallots
3 cloves garlic, minced
1 tablespoon Ras el Hanout Spice Blend (page 189)
½ teaspoon ground cumin
½ teaspoon ground coriander
1 teaspoon ground turmeric
¼ pound large red or green seedless grapes
Honey for drizzling
2 to 3 tablespoons chopped fresh cilantro

Season the chicken with salt and pepper. Place the yogurt, shallots, garlic, Ras el Hanout, cumin, coriander, and turmeric in a large bowl; mix well. Add the chicken pieces and coat well. Cover and refrigerate for a few hours, or overnight for best results.

Soak 4 to 8 wooden skewers in warm water for 1 hour. Heat the grill to medium-high or a stovetop grill pan over medium heat.

Divide the chicken pieces evenly among the skewers, threading them alternately with the grapes. Cook the chicken brochettes on an outdoor grill or the stovetop until the chicken is fully cooked and golden brown on all sides. Transfer to dinner plates, drizzle a little honey on top, and sprinkle some cilantro over all.

GRILLED LEMON AND CHICKEN BROCHETTES

Serves 4 to 8

When my grandfather set up his small outdoor grill, I knew it was time for delicious brochettes. I could hear the sizzle of chicken on the grill and smell the aroma of lemons and spices that spreads in the air. Grilled lemons take on a different taste when slightly caramelized and add a lot of citrus freshness to grilled chicken or any other meat or fish recipe. I was at the front of the line to have the first warm piece of lemon when he finished cooking.

Note: *It is best to marinate the chicken for these brochettes overnight. If you are using wooden skewers, you must soak them in warm water for at least 1 hour. If you don't have Meyer lemons, any lemon will do.*

4 skinless, boneless chicken breast halves, cut into 1½-inch cubes, patted dry with paper towels
Kosher salt
Freshly ground black pepper
Zest and juice of 1 lemon
1 shallot, minced
2 or 3 cloves garlic, minced or grated
1 to 1½ teaspoons ground ginger
1 teaspoon ground cardamom
3 to 4 tablespoons extra virgin olive oil
3 whole Meyer lemons, cut into quarters
1 or 2 tablespoons minced cilantro
Harissa (page 188)

Season the chicken with salt and pepper. Place the lemon zest and juice, shallots, garlic, ginger, cardamom, and olive oil in a large bowl; mix well. Taste for seasoning and adjust as needed. Add the chicken pieces and stir to coat well. Cover and refrigerate for a few hours, or overnight for best results.

Soak 4 to 8 wooden skewers in warm water for 1 hour. Heat the outdoor grill to medium-high or a stovetop grill pan over medium heat.

About 30 minutes before cooking the brochettes, add the Meyer lemon quarters and cilantro to the marinated chicken and mix well.

Divide the chicken pieces evenly among the skewers, threading them alternately with the lemon quarters. Cook the chicken brochettes on an outdoor grill or the grill pan until the chicken is fully cooked and golden brown on all sides. The lemon slices should be slightly caramelized. Transfer the brochettes to dinner plates and serve with Harissa. Be sure to eat the lemons with the chicken.

LIMONCELLO CHICKEN
Serves 4 to 6

Limoncello liqueur originated in the Campania region of Italy and is also made in Sicily. It is made from the skin of lemons grown in that region. It takes about three months for the limoncello to become a drinkable liqueur. The liqueur can be enjoyed as an aperitif at any meal or as an after-dinner digestive. Limoncello adds vibrant flavor to any cooked dish. In this recipe, the limoncello enhances the taste of the chicken; it's a sweet change from white wine.

Note: *Be sure the chicken is free of any water or moisture before you add it to the marinade. If it is not completely dry, it will dilute the flavors in the dish.*

4 skinless, boneless chicken breast halves, cut into 2- x 1-inch strips
Kosher salt
Freshly ground black pepper
1 pinch red pepper flakes
Zest and juice of 1 lemon
2 teaspoons minced fresh thyme leaves
2 teaspoons minced fresh rosemary leaves
6 cloves garlic, thinly sliced
3 to 4 tablespoons extra virgin olive oil
1 cup limoncello liqueur, plus more for drizzling

Dry the chicken thoroughly with paper towels and place it in a nonmetallic bowl. Season with salt and pepper. Add the red pepper flakes, lemon zest and juice, thyme, rosemary, and garlic. Stir to coat the chicken well. Cover and marinate in the refrigerator for about 2 hours.

Remove the chicken from the refrigerator about 30 minutes before cooking so that it's not so cold. Heat the oil in a large skillet over medium-high heat. Reserving the marinade, remove the chicken pieces from the marinade, shaking off any excess liquid. Carefully, so the oil doesn't spatter, cook the chicken until golden on all sides and fully cooked, 8 to 12 minutes. Do not crowd the pan; you may need to cook the chicken in batches. Transfer the chicken to a serving plate and cover. Add any remaining marinade and the limoncello to the skillet and cook to reduce the liquid for 1 to 2 minutes. Return the cooked chicken to the skillet and cook about 2 minutes in the sauce to flavor and warm the chicken. Serve warm with a drizzle of limoncello.

POTATO-CRUSTED CHICKEN

Serves 4

No, this is not the usual chicken baked with potatoes. This chicken has a much richer flavor and is enjoyably crispy. This is undoubtably a dish that children will love. Hint: Pound the chicken between two pieces of parchment. Close your eyes when you're done and feel the chicken; it's easier to determine if the thickness is uniform.

4 chicken tenderloins
Kosher salt
Freshly ground black pepper
3 large Yukon Gold potatoes, peeled
1 pinch red pepper flakes
2 to 3 tablespoons minced fresh rosemary leaves
2 tablespoons extra virgin olive oil

Using the sides of your fists, pound the chicken very thin, about ¼ inch. Dry the chicken well with paper towels until there is no liquid left. Season with salt and pepper.

Shred the potatoes on the large side of a box grater into a bowl. Add the red pepper flakes and rosemary. Season generously with salt and pepper and mix well.

Divide the potatoes into eight portions. Press one portion onto the top of each chicken piece. Gently turn the pieces over and press the remaining four portions onto the other side of the chicken.

Heat the oil in a large skillet over medium heat. When oil is hot and shimmering, carefully place the potato-crusted chicken into the pan. Do not crowd the pan; you may need to cook them in batches.

Cook until the bottom is golden brown, 3 to 4 minutes. Gently turn the chicken over once and cook until the bottom is golden brown, 3 to 4 minutes.

Tip: *It's important not to let the shredded potatoes sit out for long, or they will become watery. It's best to coat the chicken with the shredded potatoes and cook right away or you will end up with a soggy and dingy mess!*

BEEF, PORK, AND LAMB

Since consumption of pork is prohibited to Muslims in the Maghreb, lamb and beef are the most popular meats. Liver, beef heart, large intestines, kidneys, and brains, often considered the "poor relations" in the meat kingdom, are also eaten and appreciated. The best way to prepare them is to marinate them, add salt and lemon, and grill them over a charcoal fire.

In our Italian household, we ate pork and meat dishes that were made with a French, Arabic, or southern Italian influence. Many dishes in this section are a mélange à trois.

KANOUN

A *kanoun* is a low and small furnace made of clay or metal. It is used in the Maghreb by the Berbers for cooking and also as a heater. It is about sixteen inches in diameter and about eight inches deep. There are two kinds of *kanoun*: a traditional shape that has a small grill on top, and a more modern one with three indented edges that help a pot rest easily on it. It is used like a small barbecue to cook meats or tagines using coal or wood. My grandfather used the *kanoun* to cook meat brochettes and sausages.

I remember many times when my grandfather and I sat around the *kanoun* as he told me treasured stories of his younger days or of ancient legends from the Maghreb. Listening to the crackling of the fire gave me the comfort to let my imagination go. That was a long time ago, and now, I suppose, the *kanoun* is still used by the Berbers—at least I wish it to be.

TAGINE

"Tagine" is both a type of stew and the heavy clay pot it is made in. A tagine found in the Maghreb consists of two parts: a base which is flat and circular with low sides, and a large domed cover that rests inside the base ring during cooking. The cover is designed to help return all condensation to the base. Most tagine recipes instruct you to slow simmer less-expensive meats such as the neck, shoulder, or shank until it is falling off the bone. Tagines are always cooked with aromatic spices and a broth, and sometimes with lemons, olives, or vegetables.

BEEF BROCHETTES WITH CREAMY CHICKPEA SAUCE

Serves 4 to 6

Meatballs in Italy are usually cooked in a tomato sauce or in broth. In the Maghreb, there are many ways to create meatball dishes. This is a fun way to present grilled ground meat on skewers with a savory chickpea sauce.

Note: *If using an outdoor grill be sure to soak 12 to 14 wooden skewers for at least 1 hour before grilling. If using a stovetop grill, there's no need to soak ahead.*

FOR THE CHICKPEA SAUCE:
1 clove garlic, minced
Zest and juice of 1 lemon
1 pinch red pepper flakes
1 (28-ounce) can chickpeas, drained
2 tablespoons extra virgin olive oil
Kosher salt
¾ cup warm water

FOR THE BROCHETTES:
1½ pounds lean ground beef
4 cloves garlic, minced and mashed
2 large eggs
2 tablespoons finely torn fresh mint leaves
1 cup dry Italian bread crumbs
Kosher salt
Freshly ground black pepper
1 tablespoon extra virgin olive oil for skewers
1 lemon

To make the chickpea sauce: In a food processor, pulse the garlic, lemon zest, red pepper flakes, and chickpeas until the mixture is smooth. Add the lemon juice and oil, and pulse again until smooth. Season with salt if needed. Taste and adjust seasonings. If the mixture is too thick, add some warm water, a tablespoon at a time, until you have achieved the consistency of a slightly thinner hummus. Transfer to a bowl. Cover the bowl with plastic wrap and refrigerate until ready to serve.

To make the brochettes: In a large bowl, mix the beef, garlic, eggs, mint, and bread crumbs. Season with salt and pepper. Mix well. Form logs using 3 or 4 tablespoons of the beef mixture for each. Oil the skewers and thread a log onto each one.

   Grill the brochettes until golden brown on all sides, about 10 minutes. Be sure not to turn the brochettes until you can easily lift them from the grill and one side is completely golden, or the meat may stick to the grill. When ready, squeeze fresh lemon juice on top of all brochettes, transfer to a serving plate, and serve with the Creamy Chickpea Sauce.

GROUND LAMB TAGINE

Serves 4 to 6

It's important to the consistency of this dish that the lamb be coarsely ground and sautéed to golden crispy. I ask my butcher to grind it coarsely for me. Adding eggs to a tagine is customary. The eggs can be added to the dish hard-cooked, or, as in this dish, raw and beaten. Being Italian, I couldn't resist adding the grated cheese!

5 tablespoons extra virgin olive oil, divided, plus more for the pan
4 medium Yukon gold potatoes, peeled and diced
Kosher salt
Freshly ground black pepper
2 red bell peppers, ribs and seeds removed, cut in small dice
1 small red chili hot pepper, seeds removed, cut in small dice
3 tablespoons minced shallots
3 cloves garlic, minced
1½ pounds coarsely ground lamb
1 cup canned tomato puree
1 teaspoon paprika
1 teaspoon ground cinnamon
1 teaspoon ground coriander
½ teaspoon ground cumin
½ teaspoon ground cayenne
10 large eggs
½ cup grated Parmesan
3 to 4 tablespoons roughly chopped fresh Italian parsley leaves
3 to 4 tablespoons roughly torn fresh mint leaves
20 to 25 pitted and cracked green olives
Harissa (page 188) for serving

Heat the oven to 400°F. Oil a 9- x 13-inch glass pan.

Heat 3 tablespoons oil in a large skillet over medium heat. Add the potatoes; season with salt and pepper and cook until golden and soft, about 10 minutes. Transfer to a bowl and set aside. In the same skillet, sauté the bell peppers and chili peppers until golden and soft, 5 to 6 minutes. Add to the bowl with the potatoes. In the same skillet, add the remaining 2 tablespoons oil, the shallots, garlic, and ground lamb; mix well. Cook over medium-high heat until the lamb is slightly crispy and is golden, 10 to 15 minutes. Stir in the tomato puree, ½ cup water, paprika, cinnamon, coriander, cumin, and cayenne, and cook for about 5 more minutes.

In a bowl, beat the eggs and stir in the Parmesan. Season with salt and pepper. Place the potatoes and peppers in the prepared glass pan, making sure that they are spread out evenly. Next, add the lamb mixture, and spread evenly in the pan. Gently pour the egg mixture over the meat. Arrange the parsley, mint, and olives in a decorative pattern on top. Bake until the eggs are done, 20 to 25 minutes. Once ready, serve warm with a little Harissa on the side.

LAMB CHOPS WITH DRIED FIG SAUCE

Serves 4

Lamb Chops with Dried Fig Sauce highlights the delicacy and tenderness of the lamb chops. In this preparation, I added dried figs rather than fresh figs because the dried figs soften and melt into the sauce. If you love lamb and figs, you should definitely try this dish.

8 dried figs, quartered
1 cup hot water
2 tablespoons extra virgin olive oil
2 tablespoons unsalted butter, divided
8 baby lamb chops, cut from a rack, extra fat trimmed, patted dry with paper towels
Kosher salt
Freshly ground black pepper
1 large sweet onion, diced
½ cup honey
¼ cup white wine vinegar
Fresh mint leaves for garnish

Place the figs in a small bowl; add the hot water. Soak the figs for about 10 minutes to soften them.

In a large skillet, heat the oil and 1 tablespoon butter over high heat. Season the lamb chops with salt and pepper, and place them in the skillet, making sure not to overcrowd the pan. Cook in two batches, if necessary. Sear each chop for 4 to 5 minutes on each side, depending on how done you like the chops. Transfer to a plate, and cover with foil to keep warm.

In the same skillet, add the onions, reduce the heat to medium, and cook until soft and golden, 8 to 10 minutes. Allow to cool.

Reserving the water, drain the figs. Place the figs, onions, remaining 1 tablespoon butter, and honey in a food processor. Pulse until the figs are very finely chopped.

Transfer the fig mixture to the skillet. Add the vinegar and ½ cup of the fig water. Reduce the heat to medium-low. Mix well to make a sauce. If the sauce is too thick, add a little more of the fig water. Heat the sauce until it is hot; return the lamb chops to the skillet to warm with the sauce. Transfer to a platter and sprinkle fresh mint on top.

MEATBALL AND EGG TAGINE
Serves 6

Iprepare this dish in two stages: first the spicy tomato sauce and then the meatballs flavored with spices and herbs. Although I am providing measurements for the spices, how much to use is really according to your personal taste.

FOR THE SAUCE:
⅓ cup extra virgin olive oil
1 medium sweet onion, minced
2 cloves garlic, minced
1 (12-ounce) can tomato paste, reserve the empty can
½ teaspoon ground cumin
2 teaspoons granulated sugar
½ teaspoon paprika
1 pinch red pepper flakes
½ teaspoon kosher salt
¾ teaspoon freshly ground black pepper
3 tomato paste cans of warm water

FOR THE MEATBALLS:
1½ pounds lean ground beef
2 cloves garlic, minced
1 medium onion, minced
1 tablespoon extra virgin olive oil
1 cup dry Italian bread crumbs
1 teaspoon ground cumin
½ teaspoon paprika
2 to 3 tablespoons minced fresh Italian parsley or cilantro leaves
1 large egg, beaten
½ teaspoon kosher salt
½ teaspoon freshly ground black pepper

FOR THE ASSEMBLY:
6 large eggs

Crusty bread for serving

To make the sauce:

Heat the oil in a 12-inch skillet over medium heat. Add the onions, and cook until soft, 8 to 10 minutes. Add the garlic and sauté for another minute.

Add the tomato paste to the center of the pan. Mix it with the oil, garlic, and onions. Spread the tomato paste mixture out on the pan. Cook undisturbed for 3 minutes. Leaving the tomato paste to cook undisturbed helps to caramelize it, which increases the flavor of the sauce. Stir the tomato paste, then cook for another 3 minutes, undisturbed. Add the cumin, sugar, paprika, red pepper flakes, salt, and pepper. Stir well, scraping the pan.

Add the warm water and mix well again. Bring to a boil over medium heat, stir, and immediately lower the heat to a simmer. Simmer the sauce for 5 minutes. Taste the sauce for seasoning, adjust if needed.

To make the meatballs:

Combine the beef, garlic, onions, oil, bread crumbs, cumin, paprika, parsley, egg, salt, and pepper in a large bowl; mix well. Take about a tablespoon of the meatball mixture and shape it into a ball. Continue making meatballs until you have used up all of the mixture.

Assembly:

Add the meatballs to the sauce, shake the pan to bring some sauce over the meatballs. Cover, and cook for 10 minutes.

Crack the eggs into the skillet. Look for little nooks to place them in. Reduce heat to low. Cover, and cook until the eggs are done, about 8 minutes. Use a large serving spoon to scoop meatballs, an egg, and some sauce for each person. Serve with crusty bread.

TUNISIAN BEEF BROCHETTES

Serves 4 to 6

When we were growing up in Tunis, we couldn't afford steak, so we cooked with lesser quality meats that we pounded before marinating to make them tender. For this recipe, I chose sirloin steak because pounding is not required, and it is very tender and a great choice for grilling.

Note: *If you are using wooden skewers, you must soak them in warm water for at least 1 hour.*

1 ½ pounds sirloin steak
2 tablespoons Ras el Hanout Spice Blend (page 189)
1 teaspoon Harissa (page 188), plus additional for serving
1 red onion, grated
1 large clove garlic, minced
2 to 3 tablespoons minced fresh cilantro or Italian parsley leaves
3 tablespoons extra virgin olive oil
Kosher salt
Freshly ground black pepper
2 lemons

Trim the sirloin steak and cut it into 1-inch cubes.

In a large glass bowl, combine the Ras el Hanout, Harissa, onion, garlic, cilantro, and olive oil. Season with salt and pepper; mix together well. Place the beef cubes into the marinade. Massage the cubes to coat them well with the marinade. Cover and refrigerate at least 2 hours.

Thread the beef cubes onto skewers. Heat an outdoor grill to medium-high or stove top grill pan over medium heat.

Place the brochettes on the hot grill and cook for 8 to 10 minutes, uncovered. Starting at the 2-minute mark, turn the brochettes to cook another side of the cubes. Do this every 2 minutes until all four sides of the cubes have been grilled. Once cooked to your desired doneness, remove the brochettes from the grill. Transfer to a platter and squeeze one whole lemon over the top. Serve hot with slices of fresh lemon and, if desired, extra Harissa.

MERGUEZ AND EGG TAGINE

Serves 4 to 6

Merguez is a sausage widely used in Maghrebi cuisine. The name comes from the word *"mirqaz"* meaning sausage in Arabic. It is a thin spicy sausage made of lamb, beef and lamb, or, in our day, beef and mutton. It is also made with peppers and spices that give it a reddish hue. In Tunisia, *merguez* is a street food or fast food served in a sandwich adorned with harissa, onions, and other vegetables to enhance the flavor of the sausage. In this recipe, the *merguez* is accompanied by cooked vegetables and eggs and can be served as lunch or dinner. *Merguez* are now available in the US at high-end grocery stores or online.

10 *merguez*
3 tablespoons extra virgin olive oil, plus more for drizzling
1 large sweet onion, minced
2 green bell peppers, ribs and seeds removed, diced
5 Italian plum tomatoes, diced
Kosher salt
Freshly ground black pepper
4 to 6 large eggs
Crusty bread
Harissa (page 188)

Cook the sausages with a drizzle of olive oil in a large skillet over medium heat until golden on all sides, 6 to 8 minutes. Do not crowd the pan. When ready, remove from skillet and set aside.

Add the oil to the skillet and heat it over medium heat. When hot, add the onions and cook until soft and translucent, about 8 minutes. Stir in the bell peppers and cook for about 5 minutes. Add the tomatoes, season with salt and pepper, and mix well. Cook for about 2 minutes.

Return the sausages to the skillet. Bring to a simmer. If necessary, reduce heat to keep it at a simmer. Make little pockets in the sauce and crack the eggs into the pockets. Cover and simmer until the eggs are cooked, about 8 minutes.

When ready, place two or three sausages with the sauce and an egg on each dinner plate. Serve with crusty bread and Harissa on the side.

Beef, Pork, and Lamb

PORK CHOPS IN MARSALA WINE

Serves 4

Pork chops tend to dry out easily when they are cooked. To avoid this problem, marinate them beforehand and be careful not to cook them too long. To keep the chops moist and very flavorful, I add Marsala wine. I often cook with Marsala; its sweetness makes it suitable for a range of dishes, from meats to desserts. When reduced, Marsala takes on a rich, fruity, and sweeter flavor. It is also a wine I like to drink before dinner to prepare my taste buds for the meal!

4 (½-inch-thick) pork chops
6 cloves garlic: 3 cloves finely chopped, 3 cloves thinly sliced
2 tablespoons white wine vinegar
Kosher salt
Freshly ground black pepper
4 tablespoons extra virgin olive oil, divided
4 tablespoons unsalted butter, divided
6 ounces cremini or portobello mushrooms,
  or a combination, sliced
1 teaspoon minced fresh thyme leaves
1 tablespoon minced fresh rosemary leaves
½ cup Marsala wine
½ cup chicken broth

To prepare the chops: Pat the pork chops completely dry with paper towels. Using the tip of a sharp knife, create a few slits on the top, bottom, and sides of each pork chop. Place chopped garlic in each of those slits. Next, brush the pork chops with the vinegar, and sprinkle with salt and pepper.

To cook the chops: In a large heavy-bottomed skillet, heat 2 tablespoons oil and 2 tablespoons butter over medium heat until hot. For best results, cook two pork chops at a time. Add the pork chops and cook, turning once, until both sides are golden brown, 10 to 15 minutes. Timing will depend on the size of the chops and your doneness preference. When the chops are browned and done, remove them from the pan; set aside.

Heat the remaining 2 tablespoons oil and the remaining 2 tablespoons butter in the skillet over medium heat. Add the sliced garlic to the pan with the mushrooms, thyme, and rosemary. Sauté for 3 to 4 minutes. Add the wine and stir for 1 minute. Add the broth and stir for another minute. Taste for seasoning and add salt and pepper if needed.

Return the chops to the pan. Reduce heat to low, cover, and simmer for 4 to 6 minutes, turning the chops once during the simmering. The chops will soak up the rich flavors of the Marsala wine sauce. Serve warm with warm potatoes, rice, or buttered noodles.

PORK TENDERLOIN with ORANGES and FIGS

Serves 4 to 6

This pork tenderloin dish is hearty and full-flavored. The orange rind and juice add citrus notes, the spices are bright, and the figs add a subtle sweetness. For more authenticity and flavor, use a mortar and pestle instead of a food processor.

2 large oranges
¼ teaspoon kosher salt
2 cloves garlic
2 teaspoons ground coriander
2 teaspoons roughly chopped fresh rosemary leaves
½ teaspoon red pepper flakes
Freshly ground black pepper
1 (1 to 1¼-pound) pork tenderloin
1 tablespoon extra virgin olive oil, for brushing
8 large shallots, sliced in half lengthwise
8 dried figs, halved
1 cinnamon stick

Heat the oven to 450°F.

Using a vegetable peeler, remove the zest from the oranges, leaving the pith (the white part) behind. Remove any pith that may remain on the zest. Cut the zest into ½-inch strips. Squeeze the juice from the oranges into a small bowl and set that aside.

Place half of the orange zest in a small food processor, add the salt, garlic, coriander, rosemary, red pepper flakes, and 1½ teaspoons water. Season with pepper. Pulse until it becomes a paste.

Dry the pork tenderloin with paper towels. Brush the entire tenderloin with the oil. Rub the spice paste on all sides of the pork, as evenly as possible.

Place the shallots, remaining orange zest strips, figs, and cinnamon stick packed tightly toward the middle of the baking pan. Place the pork loin on top. Pour the orange juice over the pork.

Place the pan on the middle rack of the oven. Bake until the pork reaches 145°–155°F internal temperature, 20 to 25 minutes. Remove the pork from the oven, cover with aluminum foil, and let rest for 10 minutes before slicing. Remove and discard the cinnamon stick. Slice and serve with a few pieces of figs and shallots on the side.

Sausages
with Lentils
Serves 4 to 6

This dish was one of my father's favorites, especially since sausages were economical. My mother would use hot sausages because my father loved spicy food. Sausages with Lentils is a great comfort food, typical of the peasant tradition. It is a substantial dish, ideal to serve to family or friends on a cold blustery night.

2 to 3 tablespoons extra virgin olive oil
1 large onion, minced
2 cloves garlic, minced
1 carrot, shredded
1 stalk celery, minced
2 Italian sausage links, casing removed, roughly chopped
3 tablespoons tomato paste
1½ cups dry red wine
Kosher salt
Freshly ground black pepper
1 pinch red pepper flakes
2 cups chicken or vegetable broth
1½ cups cooked brown lentils

Heat the oil in a large skillet over medium heat. When hot, add the onions, garlic, carrots, and celery. Cook until soft and golden, about 10 minutes.

Move the vegetables aside and add the sausages so that they are directly on the pan. Cook until golden on all sides, about 10 minutes. Stir in the tomato paste; cook for about 1 minute. Add the wine, mix well, and cook for 2 to 3 minutes. Season with salt and pepper. Add the red pepper flakes. Mix well.

Stir in the broth and cooked lentils. Cover, and cook to combine the flavors for 5 to 8 minutes.

SICILIAN POLPETTE
WITH CAPERS
Makes 4 large or 6 small polpette

Capers give these Sicilian hamburgers a distinctive enticing taste. Even though these burgers are shaped like hamburgers, we still call them *"polpette."* It is common to add bread crumbs to the meat for meatballs; for these *polpette*, we use the bread crumbs for a coating to make a crispier burger.

1 pound lean (85 to 95%) ground beef
20 small capers in brine, drained and roughly chopped
4 cloves garlic, minced
4 tablespoons minced fresh Italian parsley leaves
1 large egg, beaten
1 pinch red pepper flakes, optional
½ cup grated pecorino or Parmesan
2 tablespoons unbleached all-purpose flour
½ cup dry white wine
Freshly ground white pepper
⅔ to 1 cup dry Italian bread crumbs
3 tablespoons olive oil
1 lemon

Place the ground beef, capers, garlic, parsley, egg, red pepper flakes, cheese, flour, and wine in a large bowl. Season with the white pepper. Gently mix well with your hands. Divide the meat mixture into 4 or 6 equal portions. Shape each portion into a patty about ½-inch thick, but no thicker.

Place the bread crumbs on a large shallow plate or bowl. Dredge each patty in the crumbs to coat. Shake off any excess bread crumbs.

Line a plate with paper towels.

Heat the oil in a large skillet over medium heat. Add the patties and cook, turning once, until golden on the outside and done to your taste. Remove to the lined plate and drain any excess oil for a few minutes. Transfer to a serving plate and squeeze fresh lemon juice on top. Serve warm.

SEAFOOD

Due to their countries' extensive coastlines, Italian and Maghrebi cuisines have always been fortunate in the diversity, quantity, and quality of fish available. Seafood recipes are numerous and delectable. The markets in the coastal cities offer a wealth of fresh fish and shellfish that can be enjoyed on site. Some of the most popular fishes and shellfish of the Maghreb are mullet, tuna, whiting, swordfish, cod, shrimp, calamari, mussels, and sardines, all of which can be baked, fried, stuffed, stewed with vegetables, or cooked with couscous.

When I was a child, seafood was on our table more often than meat. It was fairly economical and easy to purchase by simply walking over to the port section of the city of Tunis. In the mornings, seafood was sold by dozens of fishermen right from their boats. It was a place to bargain for price and quality of the day's catch. It was a great experience to have this adventure nearly every day of my childhood. It was a trip my grandfather and I enjoyed together and he taught me how to select fresh fish and how to bargain for the best price.

In this section, I include several recipes for dishes that I grew up eating. I also created some recipes that are inspired by my memories of those walks to the port.

Baked Whole Bass with Chermoula
Calamari with Peas and Garlic
Cod Frittelle with Parsley and Lemon
Cod with Tomatoes and Black Olives
Moroccan Salmon
Mussels in Tomato and Garlic Sauce
Salmon with Maghrebi Spices
Scallops in Marsala Wine and Lemon Caper Sauce
Shrimp Spiedini in Golden Bread Crumbs and Pistachios
Shrimp with Orange Sauce
Spicy Sole Croquettes
Tilapia in Pernod with Fennel

BAKED WHOLE BASS
WITH CHERMOULA
Serves 4 to 6

Baked or grilled, whole fish such as bass or branzino is almost always cooked with vegetables in the Maghreb. This seafood dish is elegant, colorful, fragrant, and a healthful way to prepare whole fish while flavoring the vegetables.

Chermoula is a marinade used in Tunisian, Moroccan, and Algerian cooking to flavor seafood, meats, and vegetables. It has the consistency of thick pesto, but it doesn't have the cheese and nuts. I often add a little harissa to the marinade because I love spicier food. This *chermoula* can be used on a baked or grilled whole fish. Baked Whole Bass with Chermoula is a stunning and elegant dish to present and serve for a special occasion.

FOR THE MARINADE *(CHERMOULA)*:
1 bunch fresh Italian parsley leaves, roughly chopped
1 bunch fresh cilantro leaves, roughly chopped
3 tablespoons extra virgin olive oil
Zest and juice of 1 lemon
2 large cloves garlic, finely minced
1 teaspoon paprika
1 teaspoon ground cumin
1 teaspoon sea salt

FOR THE FISH:
1 large sweet onion, thinly sliced
1 (2- to 3-pound) whole bass, gutted and cleaned, patted dry with paper towels
3 tablespoons extra virgin olive oil
Kosher salt
Freshly ground black pepper
4 Roma tomatoes, sliced
2 lemons, thinly sliced

FOR SERVING:
Harissa (page 188)

Heat the oven to 375°F. Line a rimmed baking sheet with parchment paper.

To make the marinade: Place the parsley, cilantro, oil, lemon zest and juice, garlic, paprika, cumin, and salt in a bowl; mix well and set aside.

To make the fish: Spread the onions on the prepared baking sheet in one layer. Rest the fish on top of the onions. Drizzle the oil on top. Season the fish with salt and pepper. Spread the marinade on the inside then the outside of the entire fish. Arrange the tomato slices and lemon slices around the fish. Bake until the fish can be flaked with a fork, 20 to 30 minutes.

To serve: Serve warm accompanied by Harissa.

Flavors of the Maghreb and Southern Italy

CALAMARI WITH PEAS AND GARLIC

Serves 4 to 6

"Calamari" is the Italian plural for *"calamaro,"* which means "squid." In many restaurants, calamari are served fried with a tomato sauce on the side. In Maghrebi cuisine, they are stuffed with rice, vegetables, or meats, cooked with vegetables, or fried in batter. Any way calamari is cooked, it is an indispensable ingredient in Maghrebi cooking. My Calamari with Peas and Garlic is a recipe my grandfather made often, especially on our ritual seafood Fridays.

2 to 3 tablespoons extra virgin olive oil
1 medium red onion, minced
3 cloves garlic, minced
1 pound small calamari, cleaned and cut with scissors into bite-size rings,
    patted dry with paper towels
2 cups frozen sweet peas, not thawed
3 tablespoons chopped fresh Italian parsley leaves, plus more for garnish
1 pinch red pepper flakes
Kosher salt
Freshly ground black pepper

Heat the oil in a large skillet over medium-low heat. Add the onions, and cook until softened, 3 to 5 minutes. Add the garlic and sauté for about 1 minute.

Raise the heat to medium-high. Add the calamari and cook, stirring occasionally, until golden, 8 to 10 minutes. Add the peas, parsley, and red pepper flakes. Season with salt and pepper. Cook until the peas are thawed. Taste for seasoning and adjust as needed. Also, taste a piece of the calamari to see if it is cooked to your liking. When ready, garnish with parsley and serve.

COD FRITTELLE WITH PARSLEY AND LEMON

Serves 4 to 6

Without a doubt, cod *frittelle* would always be at our table as one of the seven fishes courses on Christmas Eve. My mother would also make these *frittelle* for me because I didn't like to eat fish as a child, so she made the *frittelle* to conceal the fish. I like to carry on this Christmas tradition, so I make this recipe for my family on Christmas Eve. These *frittelle* are so delicious that I also make them often as an appetizer for seafood night with my husband.

2 large eggs, separated
½ teaspoon kosher salt
6 ounces cold milk
5 ounces (about 1⅜ cup) unbleached all-purpose flour
¾ teaspoon freshly ground black pepper
1 pinch red pepper flakes
Zest of 1 lemon, reserve the lemon
4 tablespoons minced fresh Italian parsley leaves, divided
1 pound cod fillets, cut in ½-inch-wide strips, patted dry with paper towels
Extra virgin olive oil for frying

In a small bowl, whisk the egg yolks with the salt. Add the milk and whisk until well combined. Set aside.

Sift the flour into a large bowl. Whisk in the pepper, red pepper flakes, lemon zest, and 2 tablespoons parsley.

Whisk the flour mixture into the yolk mixture; blend well to make a batter.

In a cold large metal bowl, using a clean dry whisk, beat the egg whites until stiff. Fold into the batter.

Add the cod to the batter, turning to coat each piece. Be sure the cod is well coated; shake off any dripping batter.

Line a baking sheet with paper towels.

Pour ¼-inch oil into a deep 12-inch skillet. Heat the oil over medium heat until hot and shimmering. Add the *frittelle* in batches, being sure not to crowd them in the pan. Cook until golden on all sides, 2 to 4 minutes on each side. When ready, transfer to the lined baking sheet to absorb any extra oil. Once all of the cod has been cooked, transfer to a serving plate. Top with the remaining 2 tablespoons parsley and a squeeze of lemon juice.

COD WITH TOMATOES AND BLACK OLIVES

Serves 4 to 6

Luckily, as an adult, I now appreciate fish. In the past few years, I've cooked cod as it was prepared by my mother so many years ago. Every time I see fresh cod at the supermarket, I buy it because I love it cooked with the tomatoes and olives. This recipe is a little Neapolitan and a little Sicilian, which is exactly what I am. I originally made this recipe the old-fashioned way with dried cod (*baccala*) which I soaked for days, changing the water several times. Dried cod can be difficult to find in stores, so I use fresh cod instead for a fresher and easier approach to this old recipe.

1½ pounds fresh cod fillets, cut into bite-size pieces, patted dry with paper towels
Kosher salt
Freshly ground black pepper
Unbleached all-purpose flour for dredging
4 tablespoons extra virgin olive oil, divided
2 cloves garlic, minced
½ to 1 teaspoon red pepper flakes
1 pint grape tomatoes, halved lengthwise
20 pitted black olives
30 capers in brine, drained
1 lemon

Season the cod with salt and pepper. Place the flour on a plate. Dredge the cod in the flour, coating well. Shake off any excess flour, or the extra flour will burn when cooking.

Line a plate with paper towels.

Heat 2 tablespoons oil in a large skillet over medium heat. Add the cod in batches; do not overcrowd the pan. Cook until golden on both sides, 3 to 5 minutes per side. Transfer the cooked cod to the lined plate to absorb any excess oil. Cover the plate and set aside.

In the same skillet, heat the remaining 2 tablespoons oil. When hot, add the garlic and red pepper flakes. Stir in the tomatoes and sauté for 5 to 6 minutes. Lastly, add the olives and capers; cook for 1 minute. Mix well. Taste for seasoning and adjust as needed.

Tuck the pieces of cod into the tomatoes in the skillet. Reduce heat to low and cook about 5 minutes, turning only once. Squeeze lemon juice over and serve warm.

MOROCCAN SALMON

Serves 4

S*aumon à la Marocaine* is a classic meal that has been around for generations. It is often cooked in Jewish homes for Shabbat. Most of us like salmon—its pink color and its delicate flavor. Because my palate prefers a spicier flavor, I cook this dish with Moroccan spices and a dollop of spicy Harissa. Adding the chickpeas makes it a complete meal. What I like about this dish is that everything can be made ahead, and at the last moment you nestle the salmon pieces in the stew and warm it up in 5 to 6 minutes. It's a dish I make often for my salmon-loving husband.

2 tablespoons extra virgin olive oil
1 large sweet onion, minced
1 (28-ounce) can chickpeas, drained
4 tablespoons tomato paste
1 pound fresh salmon, cut into 1½- x ½-inch strips, patted dry with paper towels
½ tablespoon ground cumin
½ tablespoon ground coriander
Kosher salt
Freshly ground black pepper
2 to 3 tablespoons finely chopped fresh dill
½ lemon
Harissa (page 188)

Heat the oil in a 12-inch skillet over medium-low heat. Add the onions and sauté until softened and just golden, about 10 minutes. Add the chickpeas; cook 3 minutes. Move the chickpeas and onions to the sides of the skillet, leaving a circle in the middle. Add the tomato paste to the middle of the skillet and sauté for 3 minutes, stirring occasionally. Mix everything together.

Tuck the salmon bites into the chickpea mixture. Add the cumin and coriander; season with salt and pepper. Cook for 3 minutes, gently turn the salmon, and continue cooking until the salmon becomes opaque, about 3 more minutes. Taste, and adjust seasoning if needed. Remove from the heat, top with dill and a squeeze of lemon. Serve warm with a side of Harissa.

MUSSELS IN TOMATO AND GARLIC SAUCE

Serves 4 to 6

The main ingredient in Mussels in Tomato and Garlic Sauce is the fresh mussels, which require particular attention when you purchase them. If you are not sure how fresh they are, ask your fishmonger. When I was growing up, mussels were in season only in the summer, but now they are available all year round.

Have a lot of fresh or toasted bread ready, because you will need it to mop up the delicious sauce along with these mussels.

2 dozen fresh mussels, cleaned and debearded
4 tablespoons extra virgin olive oil
4 cloves garlic, minced
1 small red hot pepper, ribs and seeds removed, minced
3 tablespoons minced fresh Italian parsley leaves
1 (28-ounce) can tomato puree
3 tablespoons tomato paste
1 cup fish stock or water
Kosher salt
Freshly ground black pepper
A large loaf of crusty bread

Check to make sure that all the mussels are closed. Discard any mussels that are open or have open cracks; they are not edible.

Place the mussels in a large saucepan over medium-high heat. Cover and cook, stirring once halfway through the cooking process, until they all open, 5 to 6 minutes. If any mussels refuse to open after cooking, discard them; they are not safe to eat. Set the cooked mussels aside.

Heat the oil in a large saucepan over medium-low heat. When hot, add the garlic, hot pepper, and parsley. Sauté for 3 to 4 minutes. Add the tomato puree, tomato paste, and stock. Season with salt and pepper. Mix well. Cook 15 minutes.

Add the mussels in their shells to the saucepan. Cook them, stirring occasionally, for 5 to 6 minutes. Remove from heat, serve in bowls with slices of bread on the side.

SALMON WITH MAGHREBI SPICES
Serves 4

Spices give a distinct flavor and scent to recipes. They should be used in small quantities to season or to add color. These salmon fillets have a unique taste because of the combination of spices selected for this dry rub. The turmeric turns it light yellow. Add a squeeze of fresh lemon juice and some Harissa on the side, and you may never eat salmon any other way!

1½ teaspoons freshly ground cumin seeds
1½ teaspoons freshly ground coriander seeds
1½ teaspoons paprika
1 teaspoon ground turmeric
½ teaspoon crushed red pepper flakes
½ teaspoon sea salt
Freshly ground black pepper
4 (6-ounce) skinless salmon fillets, patted dry with paper towels
1 tablespoon extra virgin olive oil
½ lemon
Harissa (page 188) for serving

In a small bowl, mix together the cumin, coriander, paprika, turmeric, and red pepper flakes. Season with salt and pepper. Rub the spices over all sides of the salmon fillets.

Heat the oil in a large skillet over medium-high heat; add the salmon. Cook until the salmon is lightly browned, 3 to 5 minutes. Turn over once and cook until the salmon is done to your taste, another 1 to 3 minutes. The exact cooking time depends on the thickness of the fillets. The salmon should be slightly underdone, pink in the middle. Do not overcook. When ready, squeeze fresh lemon on top, and serve Harissa on the side.

SCALLOPS IN MARSALA WINE AND LEMON CAPER SAUCE

Serves 2 to 4

The scallop, called *"capesante"* in Italian and *"Saint Jacques"* in French, is one of the most expensive shellfish. Scallops contain omega-3 fatty acids and are rich in calcium and vitamin A. The meat of scallops is so tender and sweet that it can be eaten raw as a *carpaccio* or cooked as in this light and delicate main dish. I love Marsala wine because of its sweet and intense flavor. Used in this recipe with lemons and capers, it gives a fresh and unique flavor to the scallops.

½ cup unbleached all-purpose flour, for dredging
¼ teaspoon kosher salt
1 pinch freshly ground black pepper
8 large scallops, patted dry with paper towels
4 tablespoons extra virgin olive oil, divided
2 cloves garlic, finely minced
4 tablespoons minced Italian parsley leaves, divided
2 to 3 tablespoons capers in brine, drained
½ cup Marsala wine
2 tablespoons unsalted butter
½ lemon

Place the flour, salt, and pepper on a plate. Mix well. Coat the dry scallops in the flour mixture. Shake off any excess flour, and place on a plate.

Heat a 10-inch cast-iron or heavy-bottomed skillet over medium-high heat. When hot, add 2 tablespoons oil. Heat oil for 1 minute. Add the flour-coated scallops to the pan, making sure they are far apart. Cook the scallops until golden brown, about 1 minute. Turn and cook the other side until the scallops are golden brown and crispy and beginning to firm up. Cooking time will depend on the thickness of the scallops, usually about 1 minute on each side. The middle of the scallops should be opaque. Transfer to a plate.

Reduce heat to medium-low; add remaining 2 tablespoons oil. Add the garlic, 2 tablespoons parsley, and the capers; cook for 1 minute. Add the wine and cook, whisking continually, for 2 to 3 minutes. Place the scallops and their juices into the pan with the sauce. Season with salt and pepper. Let the scallops warm for a few minutes. Stir in the butter to thicken the sauce. Remove from the heat, squeeze the lemon juice on top and sprinkle the remaining 2 tablespoons parsley on top.

SHRIMP SPIEDINI IN GOLDEN BREAD CRUMBS AND PISTACHIOS

Serves 4

This recipe appeared in *The Washington Post* and was a winning recipe in BBC Good Food magazine. I have added pistachios to the recipe and simplified the original cooking process. I just have one thing to say about this dish: what a delight!

Note: *If you are using wooden skewers, you must soak them in water for at least 1 hour.*

1 cup dry Italian bread crumbs
½ cup shelled unsalted pistachios
2 tablespoons roughly torn fresh mint leaves
Kosher salt
Freshly ground black pepper
20 large shrimp, peeled, tails left on, patted dry with paper towels

Heat the oven to 350°F. Oil a baking sheet well. If you are using wooden skewers, soak them in water for at least 1 hour.

Place the bread crumbs, pistachios, and mint in a food processor. Season with salt and pepper. Pulse until finely ground and blended. Transfer to a plate. Dredge each shrimp in the mixture to coat well, and place on a plate.

Thread 5 shrimp on each skewer. Place skewers about 1 inch apart on the prepared baking sheet. Bake, turning only once about halfway through the baking time, until golden, 5 to 8 minutes depending on size of the shrimp.

Flavors of the Maghreb and Southern Italy

SHRIMP WITH ORANGE SAUCE

Serves 4 to 6

This is a refined and delicate dish made with fresh shrimp and beautiful oranges. I make it for my Valentine's Day cooking classes and dinners—and it is relished by all. This recipe is also excellent when made with fish or scallops.

1½ pounds large shrimp, cleaned, peeled, tails left on, patted dry with paper towels
1 pinch sea salt
1 pinch freshly ground black pepper
2 tablespoons extra virgin olive oil
½ cup dry white wine
Zest and juice of 1 large orange
1 tablespoon unbleached all-purpose flour
2 tablespoons chiffonade of fresh basil leaves

Toss the shrimp, salt, and pepper together in a bowl.

Heat the oil in a large skillet over medium heat. When the oil is hot, add the shrimp and cook until the shrimp turn pink and golden on the edges, 3 to 5 minutes. Do not crowd the pan. Cook the shrimp in batches if necessary. When ready, transfer the shrimp to a plate; set aside.

Add the wine and the orange zest and juice to the skillet. Cook to reduce, about 5 minutes. Add the flour to thicken the sauce; stir well. Return the shrimp to the skillet and fold them into the sauce. Scatter the basil on top and serve warm.

SPICY SOLE CROQUETTES
Serves 4

Spicy Sole Croquettes is a peasant dish (*cucina povera*), made by fishermen at the end of the day with leftover pieces of fish from that day's catch. Today, these croquettes can be prepared easily using fresh fish or even frozen fish that has been properly thawed and is free of any liquid. They make a good entrée or appetizer served with Harissa on the side. It's a great dish to introduce to children; they will appreciate croquettes more than fish sticks.

1 pound sole fillets
2 tablespoons finely minced shallots
½ cup dry Italian bread crumbs
½ cup grated Parmesan
1 large egg
2 tablespoons finely torn fresh mint leaves
Kosher salt
Freshly ground black pepper
1 pinch red pepper flakes
Extra virgin olive oil
¾ cup unbleached all-purpose flour, for dredging
1 lemon
Harissa (page 188) for serving

Be sure that the sole is free of any liquid. If necessary, pat it dry with paper towels. Place the sole in a food processor and pulse a few times. Add the shallots, bread crumbs, Parmesan, egg, mint, ½ teaspoon salt, ¼ teaspoon pepper, and the red pepper flakes. Pulse a few more times until it looks like grains of rice.

Transfer the mixture to a bowl. Begin by testing the consistency of the sole mixture. Make a fish ball about the size of a golf ball. If it holds together well, continue using the remaining fish mixture to make balls. If the mixture is too dry, add a tiny drizzle of oil. If too wet, add a little bit of bread crumbs and Parmesan. When the mixture is ready, shape all of the fish balls. Makes 8 to 12 fish balls depending on the size.

Place the flour on a flat plate and stir in 1 pinch salt and 1 pinch pepper; mix well. Dredge the fish balls in the flour shaking off any excess flour.

Line a large plate with a double layer of paper towels.

Pour ¼ inch oil into a large skillet. Heat the oil over medium heat. When shimmering, add the fish balls about an inch apart. Do not crowd the pan. You may need to cook them in batches. Cook the fish balls until golden on all sides, 3 to 5 minutes. As they finish cooking, transfer to the prepared plate to drain off any excess oil.

Place the fish balls on a serving plate, squeeze some lemon juice on top, and serve with Harissa on the side.

TILAPIA IN PERNOD WITH FENNEL

Serves 4

Here is a French-influenced Maghrebi dish made with Pernod. Pernod is a well-known French liqueur, and a popular aperitif (cocktail) when it is mixed with cold water and ice. It is made with the essence of star anise, then mixed and distilled with essences of aromatic mint and coriander. It is often used in fish and seafood dishes, including bouillabaisse, to enhance and brighten flavors.

½ fennel bulb, greens reserved
1 tablespoon unsalted butter
2 tablespoons extra virgin olive oil
1 onion, thinly sliced
1 teaspoon ground cumin
1 teaspoon ground coriander
½ teaspoon red pepper flakes
¾ teaspoon sea salt
½ teaspoon freshly ground black pepper
4 tablespoons Pernod
Juice of ½ lemon
4 (6-ounce) tilapia fillets, patted dry with paper towels

Remove the stalks from the fennel and thinly slice the bulb; chop the fennel greens. Set both aside separately.

Melt the butter with the oil in a large skillet over medium heat. Add the onions and sauté until softened and barely golden, 8 to 10 minutes. Stir in the fennel slices and cook 3 to 4 minutes.

Add the cumin, coriander, red pepper flakes, salt, and pepper; stir and cook about 1 minute. Add the Pernod and lemon juice; stir well. Tuck the tilapia fillets in among the vegetables. Cover, and cook until the fish is turning opaque and white, about 5 minutes. Turn once; add 3 to 4 tablespoons of the reserved fennel greens, cover, and cook 2 to 3 minutes.

SALADS

In Maghrebi cuisine, salads are excellent accompaniments to baked or grilled fish, shellfish, lamb, beef, and chicken. A party is not complete without some standout salads. Maghrebi salads have complex compositions and all are made with assortments of fresh ingredients. They are made with light flavors and have intense aromas. A typical meal starts with at least one salad and, oftentimes, several. The salads that are served depend on what is available in that season and what the main dish will be. Salads are served in small portions when several are offered.

Whether you eat salad before, during, or after a meal isn't as important as what you eat. Enjoy making the salads and salad dressings in this book and when your guests come to your table, offer diverse options with the main meal. It will be the most hospitable thing you can do for your guests to express your appreciation that they joined you at your table.

Couscous "Panzanella"
Fennel, Carrot, and Orange Salad
Grilled Fennel in Balsamic Dressing
Lemony Lentil Salad
Melon and Cucumber Salad
Potato Salad with Arugula Mint Pesto
Radish Salad
Zucchini and Basil Carpaccio

DRESSINGS

Balsamic and Harissa Dressing
Fresh Lemon and Chive Dressing
Fresh Lemon, Honey, and Mint dressing
Fresh Orange and Shallot Dressing
Hummus Dressing

Couscous "Panzanella"

Serves 6 to 8

The original *panzanella* is a Tuscan poor man's dish. It's a hearty salad made with stale leftover bread that has been soaked in a little water, red onion, basil, and drizzles of olive oil and vinegar. Today, tomatoes and cucumbers are also added to this salad. I had more than my share of stale bread when I was growing up, so I prefer making it with couscous. It's a great salad to have at a cookout or a picnic on a hot summer day. It's important to give this salad some time in the refrigerator so that all of the flavors mix together well.

3 large heirloom tomatoes, diced
½ English cucumber, diced
1 red onion, thinly sliced
3 tablespoons extra virgin olive oil, divided
Kosher salt
Freshly ground black pepper
1 cup dry couscous
Zest and juice of 1 lemon
20 fresh basil leaves, in chiffonade

In a large bowl, place the tomatoes, cucumbers, onions, and 2 tablespoons oil. Season with salt and pepper.

Place the dry couscous in a large bowl and drizzle the remaining 1 tablespoon oil on top. Rub the couscous between your hands to coat the couscous with oil. You will know that the couscous is well coated if some pellets stick to your hands. Bring 2 cups of water to a boil over medium heat. Turn off the heat and add the couscous; stir well. Immediately cover the couscous with a plate for 10 minutes. When ready, fluff the couscous with a fork and transfer to the bowl with the vegetables. Mix well and refrigerate about 2 hours.

Right before serving, add the lemon zest and juice and the fresh basil. Mix well. Serve cold as a side dish or salad.

FENNEL, CARROT, AND ORANGE SALAD

Serves 6 to 8

Here's a modest salad that I make for many occasions, especially when oranges are in season and at their freshest and tastiest. The combination of fennel, orange, and carrot is very fragrant and light. I often serve this salad as an appetizer or with an entrée.

2 fennel bulbs, thinly sliced
2 medium carrots, peeled and sliced in thin rounds
1 large orange, peeled and thinly sliced in rounds
Juice of 1 large orange
2 tablespoons finely minced fresh rosemary leaves
3 to 4 tablespoons extra virgin olive oil
Kosher salt
Freshly ground black pepper

Place the fennel on a platter. Scatter the carrots over the fennel. Arrange the orange slices over the carrots.

In a small bowl, mix the orange juice with the rosemary and olive oil. Season with salt and pepper to taste. Whisk briskly to emulsify.

Pour the orange dressing over the salad. Cover and refrigerate for about 30 minutes; serve cold.

GRILLED FENNEL IN BALSAMIC DRESSING
Serves 6 to 8

Fennel is a Mediterranean plant known for its aroma and seeds. Fennel's flavor is similar to that of anise. In some wineries, fennel is offered between tastings to clear the palate. At our Sunday dinners, fennel was always available in the middle of the table to cleanse the palate between courses.

2 fennel bulbs, trimmed and sliced ½-inch thick
2 tablespoons extra virgin olive oil
Kosher salt
8 tablespoons good quality balsamic vinegar
2 tablespoons brown sugar
2 to 3 tablespoons chopped blanched almonds, toasted

Fill a large bowl with ice water. Fill a large saucepan with water and bring to a boil. Add the fennel to the boiling water and blanch about 2 minutes. Drain the fennel and immediately plunge it into the ice water. Drain well and dry with paper towels. Make sure that the fennel slices are completely dry.

Heat an outdoor grill to medium-high or a stovetop grill pan over medium heat.

Lightly brush the fennel slices with olive oil and sprinkle with salt. Grill the fennel on both sides until tender and just golden, 3 to 5 minutes. Transfer to a serving plate.

Place the vinegar and brown sugar in a small skillet over medium-low heat; stir to combine. Cook to reduce by half. Let cool slightly, then drizzle the balsamic dressing over the fennel and top with the toasted almonds.

LEMONY LENTIL SALAD

Serves 4 to 6

Lentil dishes were among the most popular foods among the poorest classes of the ancient Greek and Roman civilizations. They were considered and consumed as the poor man's meat. When we were growing up, we had lentil soup as a main course, sometimes with sausage or cut-up pieces of spaghetti. This recipe is a modern version using lentils with fresh ingredients as a salad or side dish. As a child, I was always told that lentils are a great source of iron. Somehow that stuck in my mind, so I continue to prepare them in many ways.

1 cup brown lentils, rinsed and drained, picked over to remove any debris or shriveled lentils
Kosher salt
Zest and juice of 2 lemons, divided
1 teaspoon ground coriander
½ teaspoon ground cumin
2 tablespoons extra virgin olive oil
5 scallions, finely chopped
1 cup finely chopped fresh Italian parsley or cilantro leaves
Freshly ground black pepper

Place the lentils in a large pot with 5 cups of water. Bring to a boil, cover, reduce heat to low, and simmer until the lentils are softened, about 30 minutes. About 5 minutes before the lentils are done, season with salt and add the juice of 1 lemon. Drain well.

Transfer the lentils to a serving bowl, cool, and add all of the lemon zest, the remaining lemon juice, the coriander, cumin, oil, scallions, and parsley. Season with pepper. Mix well, cover, and refrigerate for about an hour or so before serving.

MELON AND CUCUMBER SALAD

Serves 4 to 6

This melon and cucumber salad is perfect for a hot summer day. Both fruits are rich in water and mineral salt and are therefore very refreshing. You can use any kind of melon you like; I prefer cantaloupe. The rosewater provides a nice fragrance. It's a quick and mouthwatering dish that can be served as a salad, a starter, a dessert, or between courses to cleanse the palate. You can bring it to the table in a serving bowl, or you can offer it to your guests in individual elegant dishes.

2 English cucumbers, peeled
1 cantaloupe melon, seeds removed, peeled
10 to 15 fresh mint or basil leaves, in chiffonade
1½ teaspoons rosewater
Sea salt

Cut the cucumbers and melon into ¼-inch matchsticks. Place in a serving bowl and gently mix with the basil and rosewater. Season with some salt. Cover and chill for at least an hour. Serve chilled.

POTATO SALAD
WITH ARUGULA MINT PESTO

Serves 6 to 8

This potato salad is ideal for a picnic or a barbecue. The arugula and pine nuts, along with the olive oil and white wine vinegar, bring that little something more to the potatoes than the traditional mayonnaise dressing.

1 pound baby Yukon Gold potatoes, scrubbed
Kosher salt
2 cloves garlic, roughly chopped
¼ cup pine nuts, lightly toasted
2 tablespoons grated Parmesan
2 ½ cups roughly chopped baby arugula
20 fresh mint leaves
3 to 4 tablespoons extra virgin olive oil
1 tablespoon white wine vinegar
Freshly ground black pepper

Place the potatoes in a medium saucepan with enough cold water to cover them. Bring to a boil over high heat. Reduce the heat to medium-low. Add 1 tablespoon salt, partially cover the pot, and simmer until tender, 10 to 15 minutes. Drain well. Once completely cooled, cut potatoes into ½-inch slices.

In a small food processor, place the garlic, pine nuts, Parmesan, arugula, and mint. Pulse several times. Add the oil and vinegar. Season with salt and pepper; pulse several times again. The pesto should be fairly chunky, not too smooth.

Transfer the potatoes to a serving bowl; fold in the pesto. Cover and chill for an hour or two. Taste for seasoning and adjust as needed. Serve cold or at room temperature.

Radish Salad

Serves 6 to 8

Radishes are round, red, sometimes slightly streaked with white, and have a crisp white pulp inside. They are popular throughout the Maghreb. Radishes are used in salads and soups, with pasta, and even in rice dishes. Here is a simple dish that highlights the flavor of the radishes.

1 bunch radishes, shaved paper thin
3 to 4 tablespoons extra virgin olive oil
2 tablespoons white wine vinegar
2 tablespoons fresh thyme leaves
Kosher salt
Freshly ground black pepper
2 tablespoons pine nuts, lightly toasted
2 to 3 tablespoons grated Parmesan
1 tablespoon chopped fresh dill for serving, optional

Place the shaved radishes in a large bowl.

In a small bowl, whisk together 3 tablespoons oil, the vinegar, and thyme. Season with salt and pepper. Add the remaining 1 tablespoon oil to taste if desired. Pour the dressing over the radish slices and mix well. Refrigerate for about 2 hours.

When ready to serve, arrange the radish slices on a serving platter, pour any remaining dressing on top. Garnish with the toasted pine nuts, Parmesan, and dill, if using.

Tip: *Use a mandoline to very thinly slice (shave) the radishes. If you don't have a mandoline, use a vegetable peeler.*

ZUCCHINI AND BASIL CARPACCIO

Serves 4 to 6

"*Carpaccio*" is an Italian word that traditionally means very thinly sliced raw meat or fish. It now has come to include vegetables. *Carpaccio* is usually drizzled with olive oil and fresh lemon juice. For this recipe, I selected medium to smaller zucchini because they tend to be sweeter than the larger ones. Because I can't resist the temptation, I usually eat this carpaccio right away. But when I'm patient, I chill it in the refrigerator for a few hours first; it tastes more refreshing after it has chilled.

3 tablespoons extra virgin olive oil, divided
4 cloves garlic, sliced paper thin
Kosher salt
Freshly ground black pepper
2 medium zucchini, sliced into paper thin rounds
Juice of 1 large lemon
½ teaspoon paprika
2 tablespoons chopped fresh thyme leaves
2 tablespoons torn fresh basil leaves
½ cup chopped almonds, lightly toasted

Heat 1 tablespoon oil in a small frying pan over low heat. Add the garlic; season with salt and pepper. Sauté until golden, turning occasionally, about 1 minute. Set aside to cool.

Place the zucchini slices in an attractive circular pattern in one layer on a large flat serving plate. Drizzle the lemon juice on top. Sprinkle 1 teaspoon salt, ½ teaspoon pepper, the paprika, thyme, basil, and sautéed garlic over the zucchini. Drizzle remaining 2 tablespoons oil on top. Refrigerate, covered, and allow to marinate for at least an hour. Taste for seasoning and adjust as needed. Sprinkle warm almonds on top right before serving.

DRESSINGS

Dressings for Fresh Mixed Greens Salads

BALSAMIC AND HARISSA DRESSING

Makes about ½ cup

5 tablespoons extra virgin olive oil
1 tablespoon aged balsamic vinegar
1 tablespoon honey or maple syrup
¼ to ½ teaspoon Harissa (page 188)
Kosher salt
Freshly ground black pepper

Combine the olive oil, vinegar, honey, and Harissa in a small bowl. Season with salt and pepper. Whisk briskly to emulsify. Serve over fresh salad greens, grilled vegetables, fish, and seafood.

FRESH LEMON AND CHIVE DRESSING

Makes about ½ cup

Juice of 1 lemon
4 to 5 tablespoons extra virgin olive oil
Kosher salt
1 tablespoon finely chopped fresh chives

Combine the lemon juice and oil in a small bowl. Season with salt and whisk briskly to emulsify. Add the chives and mix again. Serve over fresh salad greens or grilled vegetables.

Flavors of the Maghreb and Southern Italy

FRESH LEMON, HONEY, AND MINT DRESSING

Makes about ¾ cup

2 tablespoons fresh lemon juice
3 tablespoons extra virgin olive oil
2 tablespoons finely minced scallions
2 tablespoons finely torn fresh mint leaves
2 teaspoons honey or maple syrup
2 cloves garlic, finely minced
Kosher salt
Freshly ground black pepper

Combine the lemon juice, olive oil, scallions, mint, honey, and garlic in a small bowl. Season with salt and pepper and whisk briskly to emulsify. Serve over fresh salad greens, grilled vegetables, grilled fish or seafood, or as a dressing for couscous salad.

FRESH ORANGE AND SHALLOT DRESSING

Makes about ¾ cup

Juice of 1 orange
4 to 5 tablespoons extra virgin olive oil
1 tablespoon honey or maple syrup
1 tablespoon sesame seeds, lightly toasted
½ teaspoon finely minced shallots
Kosher salt
Freshly ground black pepper

Combine the orange juice, olive oil, honey, sesame seeds, and shallots in a small bowl and whisk briskly to emulsify. Season with salt and pepper. Serve over fresh salad greens or grilled seafood.

HUMMUS DRESSING

Makes about ¾ cup

½ cup Chunky Spicy Hummus (page 15) or store-bought hummus
3 tablespoons extra virgin olive oil
2 tablespoons freshly squeezed lemon juice
Kosher salt
Freshly ground black pepper

Combine the hummus, olive oil, and lemon juice in a small bowl. Season with salt and pepper and whisk briskly to emulsify. Serve over fresh salad greens.

VEGETABLES AND SIDES

Bell Peppers in Golden Bread Crumbs
Broccoli Affogati
Chickpeas in Tomato Sauce
Eggplants Stuffed with Sharp Provolone
Escarole with Almonds and Raisins
Fennel Baked in Tomato Sauce
Grilled Eggplants in Mint and Basil Dressing
Spinach and Ricotta Polpette
Swiss Chard with Lemon and Garlic
Tomato Parmigiana
Zucchini alla Scapece
Eggplant Caponata

Maghrebi cuisine encompasses a wide selection and abundance of vegetable dishes. Vegetables are included in every aspect of a meal. I never make a meal without serving at least two vegetable dishes. I cook them in tagines, fry them, sauté them, boil them, bake them, stuff them, grill them, and roast them. There are so many methods of cooking vegetables that I could probably write a series of books. Hmmm, perhaps I will after this one!

BELL PEPPERS
in GOLDEN BREAD CRUMBS
Serves 4 to 6

Peperoni con la Mollica is a typical recipe in the Sicilian tradition that is distinguished by adding bread crumbs toward the end of the cooking. Bread crumbs were used for *cucina povera* dishes as a replacement for grated cheese, which was not readily available or affordable. Even though grated cheese is now available and affordable, I find that toasted bread crumbs actually offer more natural flavor to dishes without the saltiness of cheese. Depending on which area of Sicily, sometimes golden raisins, spicy peppers, capers, or a variety of peppers are added.

4 medium bell peppers (red, yellow, orange), ribs and seeds removed, thinly sliced
1 large sweet onion, thinly sliced
4 ripe Roma tomatoes, quartered lengthwise
5 tablespoons extra virgin olive oil, divided
½ cup dry Italian bread crumbs
½ cup grated Parmesan
3 to 4 tablespoons finely torn fresh basil leaves
Kosher salt
Freshly ground black pepper

Place the peppers, onions, and tomatoes in a large bowl. Add 3 tablespoons olive oil; mix well to coat the vegetables.

Heat a 12-inch skillet over low heat until hot. Transfer the vegetables to the skillet. Cover, and cook, turning once, until vegetables are tender, 30 to 40 minutes. The mixture will be very wet; don't worry, the bread crumbs will absorb the liquid.

Heat the remaining 2 tablespoons oil in another skillet over low heat. Add the bread crumbs and cook until golden, stirring often, 3 to 4 minutes. When golden, transfer to the skillet with the cooked vegetables. Add the Parmesan and basil; mix well. Taste, and season with salt and pepper. Serve warm or at room temperature.

BROCCOLI AFFOGATI

Serves 4 to 6

Making broccoli *affogati*, which means "suffocated broccoli," with red wine is a Catanese (from Catania, Sicily) recipe that cooks make to give this somewhat everyday vegetable incredible taste. For this recipe use a good *asciutto* (dry) Italian wine and only an aged—about two years—imported Parmigiano Reggiano, not domestic Parmesan cheese.

3 tablespoons extra virgin olive oil
4 large cloves garlic, peeled and smashed
1 pound fresh broccoli florets
1 cup dry Italian red wine
1 pinch red pepper flakes
¼ pound Parmigiano Reggiano, broken into ¼-inch pieces
Kosher salt
Freshly ground black pepper

Heat the oil in a large deep skillet over medium-low heat. When the oil is hot, add the garlic, and cook just until golden to infuse the oil, about 1 minute. Remove the garlic when golden.

Raise the heat to medium. Add the broccoli florets, and cook, stirring occasionally, about 5 minutes. Add the wine, cover, and cook another 10 minutes. Right before serving, stir in the red pepper flakes and Parmigiano. Season with salt and pepper, mix well. Cover for a few minutes to allow the cheese to melt slightly.

CHICKPEAS in TOMATO SAUCE

Serves 4 to 6

Although this dish can be somewhat soupy, it is not a soup; it's a side dish made with chickpeas, spices, and tomato paste. It is incredibly flavorful and requires little preparation. Tomato paste is used to flavor and thicken dishes as long as water isn't added. I cook my tomato paste in the middle of my skillet to allow it to caramelize. I learned this method as a child and I continue to use and teach it in my cooking classes.

2 tablespoons extra virgin olive oil
1 large sweet onion, minced
2 cloves garlic, minced
½ teaspoon ground cumin
½ teaspoon ground coriander
½ teaspoon red pepper flakes
½ teaspoon paprika
2 tablespoons tomato paste
1 pinch granulated sugar
Kosher salt
Freshly ground black pepper
1 (28-ounce) can chickpeas, drained

Heat the oil in a large skillet over medium heat. Add the onions and garlic and sauté until softened, 8 to 10 minutes. Add the cumin, coriander, red pepper flakes, and paprika, and cook for another minute.

Push the vegetables to the edges of the pan. Add the tomato paste and sugar to the center of the pan; season with salt and pepper. Cook for about 3 minutes. Add the chickpeas and 1 cup water, mix well. Cover, and cook until the sauce has somewhat thickened, 5 to 8 minutes. Taste for seasoning; adjust as needed.

Flavors of the Maghreb and Southern Italy

EGGPLANTS STUFFED WITH SHARP PROVOLONE

Serves 4 to 6

A long time ago, I used to make these elegant stuffed eggplants when I had a little more time in my schedule. After many years, I started to make them again for my husband, Bob, on Sundays at home. Whenever I make these eggplants for him, they are quick to disappear.

4 tablespoons extra virgin olive oil, divided
Kosher salt
Freshly ground black pepper
4 small Italian eggplants (about 5 to 8 inches long), halved lengthwise
4 cloves garlic, minced
3 Roma tomatoes, finely diced
½ cup dry Italian bread crumbs
3 tablespoons finely torn fresh basil leaves
2 tablespoons finely torn fresh mint leaves
1 cup grated extra sharp provolone
30 capers in brine, drained

Heat the oven to 400°F. Drizzle 1 tablespoon oil on a baking sheet. Sprinkle salt and pepper on top of the oil.

With a teaspoon, remove the pulp inside of each eggplant half, leaving about ¾-inch wall all around so that the eggplant doesn't break when it is stuffed. Reserve the pulp.

Heat 2 tablespoons oil in a large skillet over medium heat. Add the eggplant pulp, garlic, and tomatoes; sauté for 4 to 5 minutes. Transfer to a bowl. Add the bread crumbs, basil, mint, provolone, and capers. Season with salt and pepper; mix well.

Drizzle the remaining 1 tablespoon oil inside the eggplants and bake for 10 minutes.

Remove the eggplants from the oven, scoop the filling mixture into the eggplants. Return the eggplants to the oven and cook until the top of the filling is golden, 10 to 15 minutes.

ESCAROLE WITH ALMONDS AND RAISINS

Serves 4 to 6

This escarole side dish is a classic Neapolitan recipe. For me, adding almonds and raisins into a savory dish is a sweet and simple pleasure. The traditional recipe calls for pine nuts, but I prefer the taste of almonds. This escarole dish can be served not only as a side dish but also as a rich pasta sauce or as a baked topping for focaccia.

2 tablespoons golden raisins
3 tablespoons extra virgin olive oil
2 anchovies in oil, drained
2 cloves garlic, minced
1 pinch red pepper flakes
1 pound fresh escarole, roughly chopped
2 tablespoons slivered almonds or pine nuts, toasted

Soak the raisins in warm water to cover until they are softened, about 10 minutes. Drain and set aside.

Heat the oil in a large skillet over medium-high heat. When hot, add the anchovies and stir with a wooden spoon until they melt, 2 to 3 minutes. Add the garlic and red pepper flakes and sauté for about 1 minute. Add the escarole; mix well. Cover, and cook, stirring occasionally, for 15 minutes. Stir in the nuts and raisins. Remove from the heat and serve warm.

Fennel Baked in Tomato Sauce

Serves 4 to 6

Fennel is a plant with lacy greens that are also used as an herb. The bulb is crunchy and slightly sweet, with a refreshing anise flavor. Fennel can be eaten raw, battered and fried, or baked. It has a bright fresh flavor when eaten raw, sliced, with a drizzle of wine vinegar on top or with oranges as a salad. Fennel is popular throughout Mediterranean, Middle Eastern, and Asian cuisines. I make this dish for cooking demos on TV, and most viewers are astonished because they didn't know that fennel can be cooked. When I am asked, "What do you do with fennel?" I recommend this hearty Fennel Baked in Tomato Sauce every time!

Kosher salt
1 large fennel bulb, stalks and greens removed, cut in 6 to 8 wedges
2 to 3 tablespoons extra virgin olive oil
1 small carrot, peeled and minced
1 stalk celery, minced
1½ tablespoons minced shallot
½ teaspoon fresh thyme leaves
1 pinch red pepper flakes
2 cups tomato puree (*passata*)
Freshly ground black pepper
½ to ¾ cup grated Parmesan
½ to ¾ cup shredded Fontina or Gruyere

Heat the oven to 350°F.

Fill a large saucepan with water; add 1 tablespoon salt and bring to a boil. Add the fennel and boil until the fennel is tender, 6 to 8 minutes. Drain well and let cool. When cool, arrange in a deep 3-quart ovenproof casserole dish.

Heat a sauté pan over medium heat. Add the oil, carrots, celery, and shallots and sauté until barely golden, 3 to 5 minutes. Add the thyme, red pepper flakes, and tomato puree. Season with salt and pepper. Cook for 3 to 5 minutes. Taste for seasoning and adjust as needed.

Pour the sauce over the fennel, making sure to cover the fennel. Top with the Parmesan and Fontina. Bake until the cheeses have melted and the top is golden, 20 to 25 minutes.

GRILLED EGGPLANTS IN MINT AND BASIL DRESSING
Serves 4 to 6

Twice cooking the eggplants in this dish is what makes it special. The eggplants are boiled, brushed with an emulsion of extra virgin olive oil, garlic, and herbs, and then grilled. Both the cooking technique and the marinade eliminate any bitterness in the eggplants. It's important for the halves of the eggplants to be the same thickness for even cooking.

7 tablespoons extra virgin olive oil, divided
4 cloves garlic, finely minced
2 tablespoons finely torn fresh basil leaves
1 tablespoon finely torn fresh mint leaves
Kosher salt
¼ teaspoon freshly ground black pepper
4 long thin Chinese eggplants, halved lengthwise

Mix 6 tablespoons oil, garlic, basil, mint, ¼ teaspoon salt, and the pepper in a bowl. Set aside.

Bring a large pot of water to a boil over high heat. Add 1 tablespoon salt and the remaining 1 tablespoon oil. Drop in the eggplant halves, reduce heat to medium. Simmer, stirring occasionally, until just fork tender, about 3 minutes. Drain the eggplants and let cool completely. Pat dry with a clean kitchen towel.

With a sharp paring knife, slash the cut-side of each eggplant half in a crisscross pattern, about ¼-inch deep. Brush the cut-side of each eggplant generously with the oil from the herb sauce. It's okay if some herbs and garlic are on the eggplants. Sprinkle the eggplants lightly with salt.

Heat an outdoor grill to medium-high or a stove top grill pan over medium heat. Lightly oil the pan, if you are using one. Place the eggplants on the grill, skin side up, and grill until deep golden brown and cooked through, 3 to 4 minutes. Turn the eggplants over, and grill the skin side, until golden, 3 to 4 minutes. Turn only once.

Transfer to a serving plate and pour any remaining herb sauce on top.

SPINACH AND RICOTTA POLPETTE

Serves 4 to 6

These *polpette* (balls) are tasty yet easy and quick to prepare. This ricotta and spinach mixture is a classic filling used for stuffing ravioli, lasagna, cannelloni, pasta shells, tomatoes, and large mushrooms. I usually double this recipe when making any of these, so I have leftover filling to make these *polpette*. *Polpette* can also be made with meat, fish, vegetables, or a combination. The hardest thing about making this recipe is to not eat them as I prepare them.

Note: *This dish must be started the day before you are serving it, so you can drain the ricotta overnight. Draining the ricotta gets rid of excess liquid, making it thicker and creamier. (See page 198.)*

8 ounces whole milk ricotta, drained overnight
1 cup grated Parmesan, divided
8 ounces fresh spinach, rinsed, chopped, cooked, drained, and squeezed dry
1 large egg, beaten
1 cup dry Italian bread crumbs, divided
Kosher salt
Freshly ground black pepper
Extra virgin olive oil for frying
Basic Marinara Sauce (page 40), for serving

Place the drained ricotta, and ½ cup Parmesan in a large bowl; mix well until combined. Add the cooked spinach and mix well. Add the egg and ½ cup bread crumbs. Season with salt and pepper and mix well again. Cover and refrigerate the mixture for about 30 minutes.

Mix the remaining ½ cup Parmesan and the remaining ½ cup bread crumbs together on a plate. Roll the spinach mixture into balls, about 1 tablespoon each. Dredge the balls in the breadcrumb mixture.

Line a plate with a double layer of paper towels.

Pour enough oil into a large skillet to just cover the bottom. Heat the oil over medium heat. When the oil is hot, add a few balls at a time and cook until golden on all sides, 3 to 4 minutes. Do not overcrowd the pan. Drain the *polpette* on the prepared plate. Continue to cook the balls until all of the mixture has been used.

While the *polpette* are cooking, warm the marinara sauce. Serve hot with marinara sauce.

Swiss Chard
with Lemon and Garlic
Serves 4 to 6

Swiss chard is a vegetable native to the coasts of the Mediterranean Sea. It is rich in vitamin A, vitamin C, iron, calcium, potassium, and magnesium. Both the stalk and the leaves are used in many recipes. The chard can be quickly boiled and then fried in a batter. It can be added to soups, stews, pasta, and frittatas; cooked in tomato sauce; baked in pies; and much more. When boiling, the stalks need to be cooked a little longer than the leaves. Swiss Chard with Lemon and Garlic is a delicate dish that I could eat at every meal. Because it was easy to find and reasonably priced, Swiss chard was a vegetable that we ate at least two or three times a week.

- 2 bunches Swiss chard, rinsed thoroughly
- Kosher salt
- 2 to 3 tablespoons extra virgin olive oil
- 3 cloves garlic, minced
- Zest and juice of 1 lemon
- 1 pinch red pepper flakes

Tear the leaves from the stalks of the Swiss chard. Cut each stalk into two or three pieces.

Fill a medium saucepan with water, add 1 tablespoon salt and bring to a boil. Add the chard stalks first. Reduce the heat to medium and cook until al dente, about 6 minutes. Add the leaves and cook until tender, another 5 minutes. Taste for doneness or prick the stalks with a toothpick to test. When ready, drain well and cool.

In a mortar, crush the oil, garlic, lemon zest and juice, and red pepper flakes to a smooth paste. Add salt to taste; mix well.

Transfer the cooked Swiss chard to a serving plate and pour the sauce on top.

Tomato Parmigiana

Serves 4 to 6

Tomato Parmigiana is a splendid dish to make in the summertime if you are growing lots of tomatoes in your backyard. It's a unique dish to prepare in advance and serve during dinners and buffets. I make this as a treat during the holiday season because it's much simpler than making eggplant parmigiana.

4 to 5 medium ripe tomatoes, sliced
Kosher salt
Freshly ground black pepper
2 tablespoons torn fresh basil, plus more for serving
1½ cups freshly grated Parmesan, divided, plus more for sprinkling
9 ounces shredded mozzarella, divided
Extra virgin olive oil

Heat the oven to 400°F.

Arrange one-third of the tomatoes in a 9-inch square pan or a round pie pan. Season with salt and pepper. Add one-third of the basil, one-third of the Parmesan, and one-third of the mozzarella. Repeat the layers two more times.

Drizzle olive oil on top of the final layer. Sprinkle on more pepper and more Parmesan. Cover with a sheet of parchment paper and then aluminum foil. Bake for 20 minutes. Remove the parchment and foil, and bake until the top is golden, about 10 more minutes. Remove from the oven, drizzle on a little more olive oil. Add more fresh basil right before serving. Serve warm or cold.

ZUCCHINI ALLA SCAPECE

Serves 4 to 6

Zucchini *alla Scapece* is a Neapolitan dish. The zucchini is cut into rounds, fried, then marinated in vinegar. In other Italian regions, it is called "zucchini *alla poverella*," which is "zucchini peasant or poor style." Although the name might change, the recipe and process does not. The term *"scapece"* is derived from the Spanish word *"escabeche,"* the process of marinating in vinegar. *Scapece* sauce can be used on top of grilled or fried fish, seafood, and other vegetables.

4 tablespoons extra virgin olive oil, divided
2 medium zucchini, sliced into thin rounds
Kosher salt
Freshly ground black pepper
3 cloves garlic, thinly sliced
1 pinch red pepper flakes
1½ tablespoons red wine vinegar
10 to 12 fresh mint leaves, torn into tiny pieces

Heat 3 tablespoons oil in a large skillet over medium heat. When the oil is hot, add the zucchini in one layer. Be sure to spread the slices uniformly in the pan for faster and more even cooking. If you need to, you can cook them in batches. Let the slices cook, undisturbed, for a couple of minutes before turning. Cook until both sides are golden, 3 to 5 minutes per side. Transfer to a serving dish; season with salt and pepper.

Heat the remaining 1 tablespoon oil in the same skillet. Add the garlic and sauté just until golden, 45 to 60 seconds. Stir the red pepper flakes, vinegar, and mint into the garlic. Drizzle the hot dressing over the zucchini slices. Serve warm or at room temperature. The *scapece* can be refrigerated and served the next day.

EGGPLANT CAPONATA

Serves 4 to 6

This recipe is similar to the classic recipe that my mother and grandmother used to make. The difference is that I use Chinese eggplants (the long purple ones), so that I don't need to salt and drain the eggplants before cooking. I also do not add sugar to the sauce. This is a unique recipe that originated in Sicily and has been made for centuries. In different areas in Sicily there are variations using bell peppers, potatoes, oregano, and sometimes white wine.

½ cup extra virgin olive oil, divided
3 Chinese eggplants, cut in ½-inch dice
Kosher salt
Freshly ground black pepper
1 large sweet onion, cut in ½-inch dice
3 inner stalks and leaves celery, cut in ½-inch dice
15 to 20 capers in brine, drained
10 to 12 large pitted green olives, halved lengthwise
20 to 25 pine nuts, toasted
Red pepper flakes
3 cloves garlic, crushed
2 large ripe tomatoes, cut in ½-inch dice
2 to 3 tablespoons white wine vinegar
8 to 10 fresh basil leaves, roughly chopped, plus more for garnish

Heat 3 tablespoons olive oil in a large nonstick frying pan over medium heat. When the oil is hot, add the eggplant. Sauté until the eggplant is soft and has changed to a medium brown color, 10 to 15 minutes. Season with salt and pepper. Sample a piece of the eggplant to determine if it is softened and seasoned to your taste. If the eggplant taste a little crunchy, continue to cook for a few more minutes. When the eggplant is ready, remove it from the pan and place in a bowl. Set aside.

Add 2 tablespoons olive oil and the diced onion to the same pan. Sauté at medium heat until soft and slightly golden, 15 to 20 minutes. Add the chopped celery stalks and leaves, capers, olives, pine nuts, red pepper flakes, and garlic. Season with salt and pepper. Stir again until everything is tender and lightly browned, 2 to 3 minutes. Transfer to the bowl with the cooked eggplant.

If the pan is dry, add 1 tablespoon oil. Add the diced tomatoes. Let them cook, undisturbed, for a few minutes, then stir gently and season with salt and pepper. If the pan gets too dry, add another tablespoon oil. When the tomatoes are a little soft and aromatic, transfer all of the ingredients from the bowl into the frying pan with the cooked tomatoes. Over medium-high heat, quickly stir all of the ingredients while adding the vinegar. Cook for 1 to 2 minutes to allow the vinegar to reduce. Taste and season with salt and pepper, if needed, before removing from the stove.

Remove the caponata from the stove and add the fresh chopped basil. The caponata should be somewhat peppery, barely crunchy, and barely vinegary. At first bite you should be able to identify each savory ingredient. Enjoy warm or at room temperature.

PIZZA, FOCACCIA, AND STUFFED PIZZA

Thousands of years ago, humans became farmers and grew wheat. Later, they discovered they could mix wheat with water, form that mixture into discs, and roast and cook them on hot stones. This process paved the way for the creation of many types of round breads such as flat breads, pita, ufkas, focaccias, and tortillas, eventually leading to the pizzas we know today.

Pizza is not a modern food; it has been around since the 1600s. In the beginning, it was a bread dough baked in wood-fired ovens, seasoned with garlic, lard, and salt. Eventually oil replaced the lard, and, with the discovery of the tomato, the modern pizza was created. Imported from Peru to Europe by Spanish colonizers the tomato was first used in a cooked sauce with a little salt and basil. Later, someone came up with the idea of using it on pizza.

Pizza was introduced to Americans when Italians immigrated to the United States. In 1905, Gennaro Lombardi opened the first pizzeria in New York City and made the first pizza in the United States, but pizza didn't become popular for a while. During World War II, American soldiers who ate and enjoyed pizza in Italy returned with a yearning for pizza at home. These soldiers promoted the spread and popularity of pizza.

Italians are proud of their fame for giving birth to pizza. It can be made with a variety of toppings, it can be stuffed, and it doesn't always have to be round. It can be eaten in restaurants, pizzerias, or delivered to homes. My view is that the worst are found in freezers. If you want a real pizza, find a good pizzeria, or learn how to make your own. Perhaps being born in Naples has made me a pizza snob. But I invite you to try my recipes, and taste the difference for yourself!

Alba's Basic Pizza Dough

Makes 3 (10-inch) pizzas

Good pizza dough is made simply with 00 flour, water, yeast, salt, and olive oil. Some recipes call for olive oil; some do not. Some use sugar in the dough, and some do not. Although it is very easy to make the dough, a few steps are necessary in order for the dough to become elastic and soft and to rise well. Start with making the pizza dough at least 3 hours before you are going to bake it so that the dough will have a good rise. Use type 00 flour if possible. Type 00 flour is finer wheat flour typically milled in Italy; it produces a much crisper pizza crust. Use a good-quality extra virgin olive oil. Before using the yeast, make sure it is still fresh and has not expired. Add warm water to the flour and yeast; don't add the flour and yeast to the warm water. Be patient. Take your time mixing the dough. Have extra flour on hand for kneading the dough. Most important, make sure the oven is hot before placing the pizza in it. And lastly, do not put too many ingredients on the pizza if you want a crispy crust.

- 4 cups 00 flour, plus more for kneading
- 1 envelope (2¼ teaspoons) rapid rise instant yeast
- 1½ teaspoons kosher salt
- 1¾ cups warm water
- 2 tablespoons extra virgin olive oil, plus more for coating bowl

Mixing the dough: In a large bowl, whisk the flour and yeast together well. Add the salt and whisk again. Create a little well in the center of the bowl by moving the flour around.

Run the tap water to warm. Test by putting the back of your hand under the water. The water must be warm to the skin, just like testing for baby bottle formula or milk. Measure out 1¾ cups of the warm water; mix the olive oil into the water in the measuring cup. Pour a little of the liquid into the well in the flour. Gently stir it in with a wooden spoon, adding a little at a time, until all of the water is used. Mix the dough until it comes together. The dough may be a little sticky.

Sprinkle a little bit of flour on the countertop. Transfer the dough to the countertop. Dip your hands in the flour; knead the dough with your hands to form a smooth dough. If the dough appears to be a little sticky, do not add any flour to the dough; place a little flour on the countertop, and knead again. Whenever your hands stick to the dough, dip your hands in the flour. You may have to add flour often. Knead for 10 to 12 minutes. When your hands are no longer sticking to the dough, and the dough looks just a little bubbly, soft, and elastic, it is ready.

Coat another large bowl with olive oil and place the dough in the bowl. Cover with a clean kitchen cloth and let it rest in a warm area for about 3 hours.

Baking the dough: Undoubtedly, the best, and favorite, way of baking pizza is in a wood-fired oven. Since most people do not have a wood-fired oven, this is the next best way to cook it.

Heat the oven to 500°F. Use a baking stone, if available. Position the stone in the middle position of the oven. Allow the baking stone to heat up for about 20 minutes before baking. If you don't have a baking stone, use a rimmed baking sheet lined with lightly oiled parchment paper; you don't have to heat the pan ahead of time.

When the dough is ready, transfer it to the countertop. Cut the dough into 3 equal pieces. Keep the dough you are not working with covered with a clean kitchen towel. Place the dough on a piece of parchment paper. Flatten the dough with your fingertips by patting it and stretching it from the middle to the edge. Use the palms of your hands to flatten the outer edge of the dough. If the dough shrinks back in place, cover the dough with a towel, allow it to rest for 10 minutes, and try again.

When the dough is stretched to about ⅓-inch thick and 10 inches in diameter and you see a few bubbles on the surface, it's time to put the toppings on the pizza. Check to see if the dough has an even surface by closing your eyes and feeling the entire pizza with the palms of your hands. If there are some thicker sides or areas, flatten them with the palms of your hands until the surface is even. If one area is too thin, it could cook more quickly than the rest and burn.

Adding the toppings: Add the pizza toppings right before you are ready to bake it. Brush the entire pizza surface with olive oil. Add your toppings, leaving only about a ½-inch border uncovered. Be sure to spread the toppings evenly over the pizza. Transfer the pizza by sliding it onto the hot pizza stone or baking pan, and bake. Remember that too much pizza sauce will result in soggy pizza dough even at 500°F.

Freezing the dough: This recipe makes three balls of dough. Use as many as you need for a pizza or focaccia recipe and freeze the remaining balls for later use. Wrap each ball of dough tightly with plastic wrap and place it in a resealable plastic freezer bag. Remove the air, seal tightly, and freeze.

Thawing the dough: A day or two before you want to use the dough, take it out of the freezer. Remove the dough from the plastic bag and remove the plastic wrap. Place the dough in an oiled bowl, cover with plastic wrap, and place in the refrigerator. It may take up to two days to thaw. Once thawed, take the dough out of the refrigerator, cover it with a clean kitchen towel for two to three hours to bring it to room temperature before using.

Alba's Quick Pizza Sauce

Makes about 4 cups

Once you make pizza with this simple and quick sauce, you will agree that there's really no reason to order pizza out. The sauce promises to be a genuine Neapolitan sauce if made with good quality ingredients, especially the San Marzano tomatoes. Keep these ingredients in your pantry, as I do, so you can prepare your home version of Neapolitan pizza whenever you are inspired to. Make a larger batch so you can freeze it for future use, or, better yet, have a party and make lots of pizza.

Note: *Sicilian oregano can be found in Italian grocery stores. If you can't find it, use Greek or any other good quality dried oregano leaves.*

1 (28-ounce) can San Marzano tomatoes, with juice
2 tablespoons extra virgin olive oil
2 large cloves garlic, minced
½ teaspoon dried Sicilian oregano leaves
1 pinch red pepper flakes
1 tablespoon granulated sugar
Kosher salt
Freshly ground black pepper

Place the tomatoes with the juice in a food processor in 3 separate batches to avoid an overflow. Pulse until the tomatoes are crushed.

Heat the oil in a large skillet over medium-low heat. Add the garlic and cook until the garlic is golden, about 1 minute. Crush the garlic with a spatula as you are cooking it. Increase the heat to medium. Add the crushed tomatoes and cook down until the tomatoes are thick and the juice is reduced, about 10 minutes. Add the oregano, red pepper flakes, and sugar. Season with salt and pepper. Stir together and cook for about 5 minutes. You don't want pizza sauce to be too thin because it will make the pizza dough soggy. Allow to cool before using it on the pizza. It can also be stored in a glass jar in the refrigerator for later use.

FOCACCIA WITH GREEN OLIVES AND OREGANO

Serves 2 to 4

I make my focaccia with pizza dough. A focaccia is different than a pizza because it does not have sauce on top. It is usually made with one or two ingredients. Focaccia with Green Olives and Oregano is ideal to serve instead of regular bread. I cut it into small pieces and serve it to accompany a platter of cheeses and charcuterie.

1 tablespoon extra virgin olive oil, plus more for drizzling
1 ball Pizza Dough (page 152)
15 large pitted green olives, halved
1½ teaspoons dried oregano leaves
Coarse sea salt
Freshly ground black pepper

Heat the oven to 500°F. Grease a 13- x 18-inch rimmed baking sheet or a 10-inch round baking pan with 1 tablespoon oil. Stretch the pizza dough to ⅓- to ¼-inch thick on the baking sheet.

Leaving about ½-inch border, make 30 depressions in an allover pattern in the dough by pressing down gently with your thumb. Place one green olive half in each depression. Sprinkle the oregano over the top, and season with salt and pepper. Right before placing the focaccia in the oven, drizzle oil over the top.

Bake until both the bottom and top of the crust are barely golden, 10 to 15 minutes. As soon as you remove the baking sheet from the oven, drizzle additional olive oil on top.

Pizza, Focaccia, and Stuffed Pizza

PIZZA SICILIANA

Serves 4 to 6

Pizza Siciliana, which originated on the island of Sicily, is made with rich ingredients from the Maghrebi cuisine such as capers, olives, and anchovies. Pizza Siciliana is thicker than other pizzas and is usually made in a rectangle with no border. This pizza was a street food found on the boulevards of Tunis. The pizza dough filled the entire baking pan; I remember the crunchiness of every bite.

My mother learned to make this pizza as a young child. I also learned as a young child, but I could never make it to be as delicious as my mother's. Every holiday, birthday party, get-together, she would make and serve thick slices of Pizza Siciliana. I often make it for my siblings, Aldo, Janine, and Adriano; it's a nostalgic dish that takes us back to our priceless childhood memories.

4 tablespoons extra virgin olive oil, divided
2 balls Pizza Dough (page 152)
2 cups Alba's Quick Pizza Sauce (page 153)
1 small sweet onion, thinly sliced
20 pitted black olives, halved
30 capers in brine, drained
3 anchovies packed in oil, drained
Freshly ground black pepper
15 to 20 fresh basil leaves, in chiffonade

Heat the oven to 400°F. Grease a 13- x 18-inch rimmed baking sheet with 2 tablespoons oil.

Stretch the pizza dough to about 1/2-inch thick to fill the prepared baking sheet. If the dough doesn't stretch right away, allow it to rest another 20 minutes and stretch it again.

Spread the sauce over the dough, leaving no border. Sprinkle on the onions, olives, and capers. Break up the anchovies into small pieces and scatter them around the top of the pizza. Season with some pepper. Lastly, drizzle remaining 2 tablespoons oil all over the pizza.

Bake until the bottom of the crust is golden, 15 to 20 minutes. Garnish with the basil leaves.

Tip: *To cut into chiffonade, stack the basil leaves, roll them lengthwise into a cigar shape, and thinly slice crosswise.*

RUSTIC PIZZA FILLED WITH RICOTTA AND PROSCIUTTO

Serves 4 to 6

Pizza, invented centuries ago, is prepared in hundreds of versions worldwide. Undoubtedly, the best classic rustic pizza is made by Italians. This recipe, one of the best rustic pizzas, I make with two layers of dough filled with fresh ricotta and a good Italian prosciutto. For me, *Prosciutto San Daniele* is the best of the best. If I cannot find it, I buy *Prosciutto di Parma*.

Note: *This dish must be started the day before you are serving it, so you can drain the ricotta overnight. Draining the ricotta gets rid of any liquid, so the ricotta is thicker and creamier. (See page 198.)*

- 1 tablespoon extra virgin olive oil
- 2 balls Pizza Dough (page 152)
- 1 (16-ounce) container whole milk ricotta, drained overnight
- 2 large eggs, beaten
- 1 cup grated Parmesan
- 1 pinch red pepper flakes
- Freshly ground black pepper
- 8 slices prosciutto San Daniele or di Parma, finely chopped

Heat the oven to 400°F. Line a 9- x 13-inch baking sheet with parchment paper and lightly oil the paper.

Place a 12-inch piece of parchment paper on a work surface; dust it lightly with flour. Stretch one ball of dough to ⅓- to ¼-inch thick on the baking sheet. Stretch the second ball of dough to the same size on the parchment paper.

In a large bowl, mix the ricotta, eggs, Parmesan, and red pepper flakes. Season with pepper. Add the prosciutto and mix well.

Spread the ricotta mixture on the dough that is on the baking sheet, all the way to the edges. Place the second piece of pizza dough on top. There's no need to close the edges together. This is two layers of crust with a filling in between, not a pie. Take a fork and prick a few holes around the dough so it doesn't puff up and cooks evenly.

Bake until both the bottom and top of the crust are golden, 20 to 30 minutes. Cool slightly before serving. Serve it as an entrée with a salad or as an appetizer cut in squares.

RUSTIC PIZZA STUFFED WITH RED ONIONS, OLIVES, PINE NUTS, AND GOLDEN RAISINS

Serves 4 to 6

Stuffed pizzas are very popular in Southern Italy. They are usually made with leftovers and are more substantial than a pizza. Stuffed pizzas can be made ahead and reheated just before being brought to the table. This pizza is, for sure, my preferred rustic pizza pie to make. It is a feel-good pie that can be made all year round because of its readily available ingredients. What I like most are the colors and how incredibly satisfying it is at first bite.

2 balls Pizza Dough (page 158)
3 tablespoons extra virgin olive oil
3 large red onions, thinly sliced
Kosher salt
Freshly ground black pepper
1 pinch red pepper flakes
½ teaspoon dried oregano leaves
20 whole pitted black olives
2 tablespoons golden raisins
2 tablespoons pine nuts, toasted
½ cup freshly grated pecorino

Heat the oven to 400°F. Place two 12-inch pieces of parchment paper on a work surface; dust them lightly with flour. Stretch the two balls of pizza dough to 8-inch circles on the parchment paper.

Heat the oil in a large skillet over medium-low heat. When hot, add the onions and cook until soft and slightly golden, 20 to 25 minutes. Season with salt and pepper. Add the red pepper flakes and oregano. Stir to mix well. Add the olives, raisins, and pine nuts. Gently fold together.

Place one of the pizza doughs in a 9-inch glass pie pan. Spread the onion mixture evenly on the dough. Top with the grated pecorino.

Place the second pizza dough on top. Cut off any extra dough from the sides of the pie plate, leaving enough dough to be able to fold the bottom and top dough together. Prick holes with a fork all over the top of the pie so it doesn't puff up and fold edges together.

Bake until the entire crust is golden, 30 to 40 minutes. Cool slightly before serving.

SAVORY VEGETABLE PIE

Serves 4 to 6

Called *"erbazzone"* in Italy this is a savory thin flat pie that is stuffed with fresh raw vegetables. I use Swiss chard and spinach, but, if you prefer, you can use Tuscan kale—try mixing them up or use only one or two. I make this dish often whenever my friend, who owns an organic farm close by, grows Swiss chard and spinach. Freshly picked greens from the farm have an exceptional flavor. This is a popular recipe with origins in the Emilia-Romagna region in Italy, where the greens are cooked with onions, garlic, and cheese. My version, which my mother made, is much easier and fresher—the best part about my recipe is that I do not cook the vegetables before baking the pie. When it is baking in your oven; the wonderful scent will spread throughout your kitchen. Serve it for breakfast, or as a snack or appetizer.

Note: *You can use only one type of greens in this pie or a combination of two or three.*

8 ounces baby spinach, Swiss chard, or Tuscan kale leaves
2 sheets puff pastry dough, thawed in the refrigerator
1 large shallot, very thinly sliced
2 cloves garlic, thinly sliced
½ cup grated Parmesan cheese
Freshly ground black pepper
Red pepper flakes
2 to 3 tablespoons extra virgin olive oil, divided

Heat the oven to 400°F. Line a 13- x 18-inch rimmed baking sheet with parchment paper.

Using your hands, tear the greens into a bowl. Reserve the stalks for soup or another recipe.

Place 1 sheet of cold puff pastry dough on the parchment paper, slightly pressing down to make sure it is even. Spread the spinach and Swiss chard leaves evenly over the dough, pressing them down slightly, and leaving about a half-inch border. Sprinkle the shallot slices and garlic over the top. Add the grated cheese, and season with black pepper and red pepper flakes. Lastly drizzle 2 tablespoons olive oil on top.

Place the second layer of dough on top and crimp the edges together with a fork or roll it over to close the edges. Now prick the top layer all over with a fork; make sure to go all the way through the top pastry, otherwise the dough will puff up when baked. Use a pastry brush to brush the remaining 1 tablespoon olive oil on top of the pie crust.

Bake until the top is lightly golden, about 30 minutes. Let the *erbazzone* cool. Cut it into squares and serve it warm or at room temperature.

SIMPLE FOCACCIA WITH FRESH ROSEMARY AND SEA SALT

Serves 2 to 4

Practically everyone likes this rosemary focaccia. Use it as sandwich bread or serve it as an appetizer course for a special supper, accompanied by cheeses and Italian cold cuts like salami, prosciutto, and mortadella. A focaccia is a little thicker and softer than a pizza. It is usually made with 1 or 2 ingredients plus sea salt, and a good drizzle of good quality extra virgin olive oil. While the focaccia is baking, it is difficult for me to resist the enticing yeasty fragrance of the dough and the warm scent of fresh rosemary.

3 tablespoons extra virgin olive oil, plus more for pan
1 ball Pizza Dough (page 152)
2 tablespoons roughly chopped fresh rosemary leaves
Sea salt

Heat the oven to 500°F.

Drizzle some oil on a 13- x 18-inch rimmed baking sheet. Stretch the pizza dough evenly on the baking sheet. Dough should be flat and even all over, with no thick border. Sprinkle the rosemary and some sea salt evenly over the dough. Right before placing the focaccia in the oven, drizzle the oil over the top. Bake until both the bottom and the top of the crust are golden, 10 to 15 minutes. Drizzle olive oil on top.

PIZZA ALLA MARGHERITA

In the summer of 1889, King Umberto I and Queen Margherita spent the summer in Naples. The queen became very curious about pizza. She had never eaten it but had heard much about it through writings or from artists admitted to the court. As a queen, she could not go directly to the pizzeria, so she summoned Don Raffaele, the pizzeria owner, to her. Don Raffaele decided to make his special pizza with mozzarella, tomato, and basil in honor of Queen Margherita's visit. This pizza was already known in Naples, but nobody had given it a name. Although the ingredients were the colors of the Italian flag, Don Raffaele did not use them for patriotic reasons. The next day, Don Raffaele took advantage of this opportunity and listed this pizza as "Pizza alla Margherita" at his pizzeria. Across Italy, everyone began talking about and eating pizza Margherita.

TUNISIAN STREET FOOD PIZZA

Serves 4 to 6

Pizza was a common street food in Tunis. My father would take us for long walks on Sundays and we would always stop for a slice of pizza. Besides the Sicilian pizza, this is one of the pizzas my father preferred. I loved it too; however, I didn't like it with the tuna on top. Now when I make it, which is often because I have a pizza oven, I tend to like it with tuna.

2 tablespoons extra virgin olive oil, plus more for the pan
2 balls Pizza Dough (page 152)
2 cups Alba's Quick Pizza Sauce (page 153)
¼ to ½ teaspoon dried oregano leaves
2 large balls mozzarella in brine, drained and pulled apart by hand
20 to 25 black oil-cured pitted Moroccan olives
Kosher salt
Freshly ground black pepper
Red pepper flakes
2 (5-ounce) cans Italian tuna in olive oil, drained
Harissa (page 188) for serving

Heat the oven to 400°F. Line a 9- x 13-inch baking sheet with parchment paper and lightly oil the paper.

Combine the two pizza dough balls and stretch the dough to about ⅓-inch thick, to fill the prepared baking sheet. If the dough doesn't stretch right away, allow it to rest another 20 minutes and stretch it again.

Spread the sauce over the dough, leaving no border. Sprinkle on the oregano. Top with the mozzarella. Place the olives over the entire pizza. Season with salt, pepper, and red pepper flakes. Lastly, drizzle the remaining 2 tablespoons oil all over the pizza.

Bake until the bottom of the crust is golden, 15 to 20 minutes. Serve each slice topped with a few pieces of tuna and a dollop of harissa.

EGGS AND FRITTATAS

Easter Pie

Eggs in a Cage

Eggs in a Skillet with Tomatoes

Frittata with Fresh Herbs and Shallots

Mini Frittatas with Peas and Mint

Mini Frittatas with Zucchini and Pine Nuts

Frittata di Pasta

The classic Italian frittata is a hearty, yet simple, dish made from eggs and enriched with a variety of ingredients. The word "frittata" is derived from the Latin word *"frixura,"* which means fried. The frittata originated in Italy and is similar to a French omelet. The difference is that the ingredients in the frittata are mixed with the eggs before they are cooked, while in a French omelet, the ingredients are tucked into the eggs after they are cooked. A frittata can be eaten for breakfast, lunch, or dinner and can be served as an appetizer, main dish, side dish, or dessert. It can even be eaten cold.

The frittata is an old *contadina*, or peasant dish, dating back to at least the Roman times. In Roman times, it was typically made with leftovers such as lettuce, rose petals, and meats. Today, the frittata is made with a wide variety of vegetables, meats, and even leftover pasta with a nice sprinkling of grated cheese. It is sometimes served inside bread to make a *frittata panino*, which is what my grandmother gave us for our school lunches.

The method of making a frittata is easy: Just break the eggs into a bowl, add salt and pepper, and whisk together. Add herbs, cheese, or cooked meats; mix well. Heat a little oil or butter in a pan, then pour the egg mixture into the pan, and cook over a medium-low heat. When the frittata is golden on the bottom, turn it over, and cook until golden on the other side.

Here are some easy tips for a successful frittata: Do not overbeat the eggs, beat only until the egg whites and yolks are mixed; this keeps the eggs fluffier. Have the pan very hot when the egg mixture is poured in, then lower the heat to allow the frittata to cook in its own time. Lastly, flip the frittata only once when the bottom is golden.

EASTER PIE

Serves 4 to 8

*T*orta Pasqualina, Easter Pie, is said to have originated around the fifteenth century in Genoa, Italy. It was, and still is, eaten during the Easter season. It is traditionally made with Swiss chard and hard-cooked eggs. I prefer Swiss chard, but when I can't find it, I use spinach.

Note: *This dish must be started the day before you are serving it, so you can drain the ricotta overnight. Draining the ricotta gets rid of any liquid, so the ricotta is thicker and creamier. (See page 198.)*

1½ pounds fresh Swiss chard or spinach, or frozen spinach, thawed and squeezed dry
Kosher salt
3 tablespoons extra virgin olive oil, plus more for drizzling
2 cloves garlic, minced
1 tablespoon minced fresh marjoram
Freshly ground black pepper
1 pound whole milk ricotta, drained overnight
1½ cups grated Parmesan, divided
Unbleached all-purpose flour for dusting
2 pieces store-bought puff pastry, thawed in the refrigerator
4 or 5 large eggs, plus 1 large egg for brushing

Heat the oven to 350°F.

If you are using the fresh greens, fill a medium skillet with water; add 1 teaspoon salt, and bring to a boil. When the water boils, add the greens. After they have cooked for a few minutes, drain it well. Set aside until cool enough to handle, then squeeze out all of the liquid with your hands.

In a large skillet, heat 3 tablespoons oil over medium heat. Add the garlic and cook until barely golden, about 1 minute. Add the greens and marjoram. Add 1 pinch salt; season with pepper. Cook, stirring, until the greens are completely dry, 2 to 3 minutes. Cool slightly.

In a large bowl, whisk the ricotta for about 1 minute. Add the greens mixture and mix well. Season with salt and pepper. Add ¾ cup Parmesan and mix well.

Dust a work surface lightly with flour. With a rolling pin, roll and lightly stretch one piece of cold puff pastry to fit the bottom and up the sides of a 10-inch pie pan. Place the pastry in the pie pan. Prick the bottom of the puff pastry several times with a fork. Spoon the ricotta mixture evenly on the pastry. Spread the remaining ¾ cup Parmesan on top. Holding a soup spoon with the handle toward the outside of the pan, make 4 or 5 indentations around the pie. Make each indentation deep enough to hold one egg, about ½ inch. Crack an egg into a small glass, and gently pour it into one indentation. It is okay if some of the white runs over the edge of the indentation. Repeat with the remaining 3 eggs. Sprinkle pepper over each egg. Drizzle a drop or two of olive oil on top of each egg.

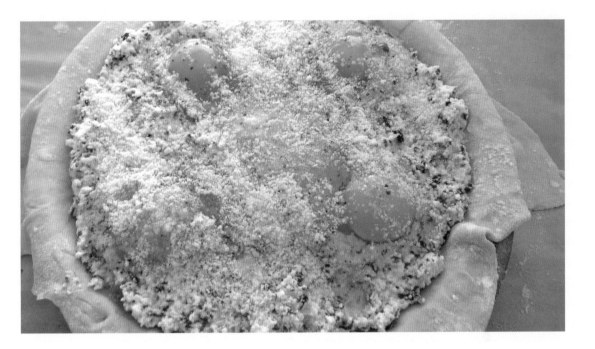

Lightly stretch the second puff pastry dough and place it on top of the pie. Cut off the excess dough, leaving about ½ inch extending over the baking dish. Fold the bottom and top puff pastry layers toward the inside of the pan, closing the entire pie. Pinch the two pieces of pastry together to seal the pie. Cut a tiny hole in the middle of the pie to allow the steam to vent. If there is excess dough, you can make pretty shapes with it to decorate the top of the pie.

Beat the remaining egg, and lightly brush it over the top of the pie. Bake until the pie is golden on top, about 50 minutes. Allow to rest for 10 to 15 minutes before serving.

EGGS IN A CAGE
Serves 2

This is another *cucina povera* recipe that was very popular in my childhood. It was made with a slice of day-old bread that had a hole cut out of the center so the egg could be nestled in. It was then quickly fried in olive oil and flipped once. When it was time to eat, I looked forward to having the egg yolk ooze out, so I could dip the crusty hot bread in it. Today, many kinds of gourmet breads are used and other ingredients are added to modernize this recipe. I like this old-fashioned version as is.

2 slices rustic bread, about ½-inch thick
2 tablespoons extra virgin olive oil
2 large eggs
Kosher salt
Freshly ground black pepper

Cut a circle out of the middle of each slice of bread with a knife or biscuit cutter. Cut just enough to make room for the egg.

Warm the olive oil in a nonstick skillet over medium heat. When hot, add the bread. Crack an egg into a small glass, and gently pour it into the hole of each slice of bread, being careful not to break the yolks. Sprinkle with salt and pepper. Allow to cook until the egg is white on the bottom. Carefully flip and let the egg white finish cooking on the other side.

EGGS IN A SKILLET WITH TOMATOES

Serves 4

This is a classic recipe that I enjoyed many times when I was a child. When I eat this dish, it evokes childhood memories and warms my heart thinking of my grandparents or my mother preparing it for me. I looked forward to eating it because I loved doing the *"scarpeta,"* which means scooping sauce with bread. I looked forward to dipping day-old bread in the egg yolks while scooping up some of the tomato. I'll sometimes make this dish just for me, so I can enjoy that feeling of stepping back in time.

2 to 3 tablespoons extra virgin olive oil
2 cloves garlic, thinly sliced
2 large ripe tomatoes, sliced in ½-inch rounds
Kosher salt
Freshly ground black pepper
1 pinch red pepper flakes
4 large eggs
Slices of hearty day-old bread

Heat the oil in a medium skillet over medium-low heat. When the oil is hot, add the garlic and cook until just golden, 30 to 45 seconds. Carefully add the tomato slices; the oil may spatter. Season with salt and pepper and add the red pepper flakes. Cook until just golden on both sides, about 5 minutes a side, flipping them once.

Create four nooks among the tomato slices and crack the eggs into the nooks. Cover, and cook until the whites are firm, but the yolks are still runny, 10 to 12 minutes. When ready, grind fresh pepper over the eggs, and serve them warm with the bread to dip in the yolks.

FRITTATA WITH FRESH HERBS AND SHALLOTS
Serves 4 to 6

I have a passion for using refreshing mixed herbs in dishes—why not put them in a frittata? I grow many types of herbs in the summer to use in my recipes. Since I love eggs, and I love herbs, this is a good dish to marry the two ingredients. My other love is cheese, so I sneak that in to spice this up a bit!

3 tablespoons extra virgin olive oil, divided
3 tablespoons thinly sliced shallots
Kosher salt
Freshly ground black pepper
6 large eggs
½ cup grated pecorino
2 tablespoons finely torn fresh basil leaves
2 tablespoons finely torn fresh mint leaves
2 tablespoons minced fresh dill
2 tablespoons minced fresh Italian parsley leaves
2 tablespoons minced fresh thyme leaves
2 tablespoons minced fresh chives

Heat 2 tablespoons olive oil in a nonstick 8-inch skillet over medium heat. When hot, add the shallots and cook until soft and translucent, 6 to 8 minutes. Season with salt and pepper. Set aside to cool.

Beat the eggs and pecorino together in a bowl. Add the shallots and herbs; mix gently.

In the same skillet, heat the remaining 1 tablespoon olive oil over medium-high heat. When hot, add the egg mixture. Lower the heat to medium-low. Cook the frittata until golden brown on both sides, 6 to 8 minutes on each side.

Note: *You can also make mini frittatas by dividing the mixture into two to three portions and using a 4-inch or 6-inch skillet.*

MINI FRITTATAS WITH PEAS AND MINT

Serves 4 to 6

Here's a recipe for a frittata with sweet peas and mint that little chefs will enjoy making and eating. It is a more healthful alternative to potatoes or heavy frittatas. For the little chefs, mini or pancake-size small frittatas are more fun to make and easier to eat. I do not add salt to this recipe because I don't like to mask the taste of the sweet peas. If you prefer, you can make one large frittata.

6 large eggs
2 tablespoons whole milk ricotta, well drained (see page 198)
½ cup grated Parmesan
1 pinch red pepper flakes, optional
Freshly ground black pepper
1½ cups frozen sweet peas, thawed and drained
2 to 3 tablespoons finely torn fresh mint
1 tablespoon extra virgin olive oil

In a large bowl, beat the eggs, ricotta, Parmesan, red pepper flakes if using, and black pepper to taste. Add the peas and mint; mix well.

Heat the olive oil in a 10-inch nonstick skillet over medium-high heat. Ladle in the egg mixture, about ¼ cup for each frittata. You will need to make the frittatas in batches, two or three at a time. Do not crowd them in the pan. Cook the frittata(s) until the bottom is golden brown, 2 to 3 minutes. Flip and cook the other side to golden brown, another 2 to 3 minutes. If the pan gets too dry, drizzle in ½ tablespoon oil. Enjoy hot or at room temperature.

MINI FRITTATAS WITH ZUCCHINI AND PINE NUTS

Serves 4 to 6

Easy and fresh tasting, this frittata with zucchini is best eaten at room temperature. Eat it with a salad, soup, a plate of pungent cheeses, or just cut in little squares and served as an appetizer. My grandfather made it with fresh mint and not the pine nuts. Sometimes I make it my grandfather's way, and sometimes I make it this way—all good!

Note: *Once the zucchini is grated, be sure to cook it in the frittata right away, or the zucchini will get soggy.*

3 tablespoons extra virgin olive oil, divided, plus more if needed for the pan
1 medium red onion, thinly sliced
2 medium zucchini, shredded
Kosher salt
Freshly ground black pepper
6 large eggs
½ cup grated pecorino
1 tablespoon finely minced fresh rosemary leaves
3 tablespoons pine nuts, lightly toasted

Heat 2 tablespoons olive oil in a 12-inch nonstick skillet over medium heat. When hot, add the onions, and cook until soft and translucent, 6 to 8 minutes. Add the zucchini and cook, stirring occasionally, until golden, 10 to 12 minutes, Season with salt and pepper. Set aside to cool.

In a large bowl, beat the eggs, pecorino, and rosemary until well combined. Add the cooled zucchini mixture and pine nuts; mix gently.

Heat the remaining 1 tablespoon olive oil in the same skillet over medium heat. Ladle in the egg mixture, about ¼ cup for each frittata. You will need to make the frittatas in batches, two or three at a time. Do not crowd them in the pan. Cook the frittatas until the bottoms are golden brown, 2 to 3 minutes. Flip and cook the other side to golden brown, another 2 to 3 minutes. If the pan gets too dry, add ½ tablespoon oil.

Tip: *Lightly toast the pine nuts in a dry pan over low heat.*

Flavors of the Maghreb and Southern Italy

Frittata di Pasta

Serves 4 to 6

My family would have this frittata the day after we had pasta to economize on food. Now, when I make a pasta dish, I make sure I have leftovers to make this dish. I like to cook mine a couple more minutes on each side so it's even crispier.

Note: *If you have extra pasta sauce from the day before do not add it to the frittata. But you can serve it as a side sauce with the frittata if you wish.*

6 large eggs, lightly beaten
Kosher salt
Freshly ground black pepper
Red pepper flakes
½ pound leftover cooked pasta in spaghetti sauce, pesto, or meat sauce
½ to ¾ cup grated pecorino or Parmesan cheese, plus more for garnish
6 to 8 fresh basil leaves, roughly chopped, plus more for garnish
2 tablespoons extra virgin olive oil

Beat the eggs in a large bowl with a sprinkling of salt, pepper, and red pepper flakes. Fold in the leftover pasta. Make sure the pasta is fully incorporated with the beaten eggs. Add the grated cheese and basil, and fold again.

Heat the olive oil in a medium nonstick frying pan over medium heat. When the oil is hot, pour the spaghetti mixture into the pan and flatten it out evenly. Cook the frittata, undisturbed. After 8 minutes, check the bottom of the frittata to see if it is golden brown; the top should be partially set. If it appears a bit uncooked, cook for an additional minute or two. Once golden on the bottom, it is time to flip it and cook the other side. Flip it carefully. You can flip it by covering the pan with a plate larger than the frying pan. Flip the frittata from the frying pan onto the plate. Then slide the frittata back into the pan with the uncooked side down and cook until that side is golden and slightly crispy.

Once the frittata is golden on both sides, place on a serving plate and sprinkle with additional grated cheese and fresh basil. Serve warm or at room temperature.

DESSERTS

Our meals are not complete without indulging in a sweet bite of Maghrebi dessert. The table is filled with an array of colorful stuffed dates, figs, fruit bathed in wine, and pastries in delicate flower water and honey. At our home, we prepared desserts days ahead for holidays and special occasions. After dinner, we all cleared the table to make room for the desserts that were coming. I was a child who loved dessert more than any food. I, along with everyone else, looked forward to this portion of the meal and took the time to gaze at the sweet delights before partaking.

Date and Almond Milk Smoothie
Marzipan-Stuffed Dates
Focaccia with Cannoli Topping
Fresh Peach and Rosemary Focaccia
Fried Pizza Dough with Cinnamon Sugar
Apricot Crostata
Pears Stuffed with Ricotta and Honey
Puckery Lemon Cake
Ricotta and Espresso Dessert

DATES

"The Fountain of Life Tree"

Date palms, which produce the exotic dates, are among the most ancient fruit trees in the world. These fruits have fed people who live in the Sahara Desert, from Morocco up to the Persian Gulf, for centuries. The Arabs consider this tree a sacred plant; they call it "the fountain of life" and "the blessed" because this tree offers plentiful fruits.

The date palm begins to bear fruit after the third year and can live for over 300 years. An average date palm produces around 100 pounds of fruit a year. For the Egyptians, the date palm was a symbol of fertility. The Greeks and Romans used the leaves as ornaments during triumphant celebrations. In the Christian tradition, the date palm became a symbol of peace and is tied today to Easter.

Dates have either a hard or soft flesh. The hard flesh variety is known mostly in Arab countries; the soft fleshy dates are appreciated predominantly in European and American countries. The best time to eat fresh dates is when they are in season and are fresh and full of water. Dried dates are available year-round. Dates are either sun dried in the open air for ten to fifteen days or dried in ovens or dryers. The fresh dates contain half the calories of dried dates. I proudly display dates on my table on festive occasions and during the holiday season.

DATE AND ALMOND MILK SMOOTHIE

Serves 4

A refreshing cool smoothie made with Deglet Noor dates. Deglet dates, found in the Mediterranean region, are soft and have a honey-like taste. Honey or sugar is not required for this or any other smoothies when you use these dates!

Note: *Keep Deglet Noor dates in a cool place. You can even freeze them so they will last a long time.*

20 soft pitted Deglet dates
4 cups cold almond milk
1 banana, roughly chopped

Place the dates, almond milk, and banana in a blender, and blend until smooth (there may be tiny pieces of dates). Pour into tall glasses and serve cold.

MARZIPAN-STUFFED DATES

Makes 30

These are typical Maghrebi sweets that are filled with marzipan. I make these around the Christmas holiday because they are so colorful. Traditionally, these dates are filled with marzipan that has food coloring added to it to show off the contrasting colors that are typical of the Maghrebi table. There's no cooking involved; just a little work is needed to incorporate the food coloring into the marzipan—it's worth the wait. Hint: When you mix the food coloring into the marzipan, you may want to wear gloves, so your hands do not get stained.

Note: *If you use dates that are not already pitted, just make a small slit, and pull out the pit.*

30 large pitted Medjool dates
1 cup marzipan
1 teaspoon rosewater
1 small drop red food coloring
1 small drop green food coloring
Granulated sugar for dipping, optional

Open up the dates to make room for the stuffing; set aside.

Soften the marzipan by adding the rosewater, a few drops at a time; mix well.

Divide the marzipan equally into three portions; place each portion in a different small bowl. Set one bowl aside; that portion will remain the natural color. Add 1 drop red food coloring to the portion in the second bowl; mix well with your hands, kneading until the food coloring is well incorporated; sometimes it takes 5 minutes. Wash hands well or change your gloves, so the color is not transferred to the other bowls of marzipan. Add a drop of green food coloring to the third bowl; mix well with your hands, kneading until the food coloring is well incorporated, about 5 minutes. Wash hands well.

Pinch off about 1 teaspoon marzipan mixture and roll it between your palms to shape it into an oval. Stuff it into a date. Continue stuffing the dates until all of the marzipan is used.

If you are using the sugar topping, pour the sugar onto a flat plate. Quickly dip the filling of the stuffed dates in the granulated sugar. Arrange on a platter and serve.

FOCACCIA WITH CANNOLI TOPPING
Serves 4

This is a simpler alternative to making and filling cannoli shells. Make the cannoli filling and refrigerate it. While the filling is in the refrigerator, make a simple focaccia. When the focaccia has been baked and cooled, spread that delectable filling over the focaccia and serve. You may need to make more than one.

Note: *For this recipe, the ricotta must be drained the night before to get rid of any liquid so it will be creamy when ready to use. If the ricotta is not drained, the focaccia may be soggy. (See page 198.)*
Be sure to rest the dough in a covered oiled bowl for 2 to 3 hours at room temperature to rise before you use it.

FOR THE RICOTTA FILLING:
1 (15-ounce) container whole milk ricotta, drained overnight
1 tablespoon pure vanilla extract
1 cup confectioners' sugar
Grated zest of 1 medium orange
¼ cup mini chocolate chips

FOR THE ASSEMBLY:
1 ball Pizza Dough (page 152), rested in a bowl for 2 to 3 hours
Extra virgin olive oil for brushing

To make the ricotta filling: Mix together ricotta, vanilla, confectioners' sugar, orange zest, and chocolate chips in a bowl. Cover and refrigerate until ready to use.

Assembly: Heat the oven to 500°F.

Using your fingertips, stretch the pizza dough evenly to ½-inch thick on a 13- x 18-inch baking sheet. Dough should be flat and even all over, with no thick border. If the dough resists the stretching, allow it to rest 20 minutes and try again once it has relaxed.

Lightly brush the dough all over with oil. Bake until both the bottom and top of the crust are golden, 10 to 15 minutes.

Let the crust cool completely.

Spread the ricotta filling over the entire crust, all the way to the edges. Cut into wedges to serve.

FRESH PEACH AND ROSEMARY FOCACCIA

Serves 4 to 6

If you are looking for something simple and sweet to bake, try this Focaccia with Fresh Peaches and Rosemary—it's a creative way to use pizza dough. This focaccia can be made with a variety of fresh fruits; grapes, figs, and plums are especially good. My favorite fruit to use in this dessert focaccia is fresh summer peaches.

1 ball Pizza Dough (page 152) or ready-made pizza dough, at room temperature
1 tablespoon extra virgin olive oil, plus more for the pan
2 large peaches, skin and pits removed, thinly sliced
1 tablespoon minced fresh rosemary leaves
2 tablespoons granulated sugar
1 pinch sea salt
1 pinch black pepper

Place the pizza dough in a bowl. Cover and let sit at room temperature for 2 to 3 hours.

Heat the oven to 425°F. Rub a little olive oil on a 13- x 18-inch baking sheet.

Transfer the dough to the baking sheet and stretch it, pressing with your fingertips. Stretch the dough until it is about ¼-inch thick. It can be oval, round, or rustic shape. If the dough keeps shrinking when you stop pressing on it, let it rest for 15 to 20 minutes. Quickly arrange the

sliced peaches, about ¼-inch apart, in a decorative pattern on the dough. Sprinkle with the rosemary; drizzle 1 tablespoon oil on top, making sure to drizzle some around the edges. Finish by sprinkling the sugar, salt, and pepper evenly on top.

Bake until both the bottom and the top of the crust are golden, 20 to 30 minutes.

Tip: *If you want to make sure the dough's thickness is uniform, close your eyes and feel it. You will be much more accurate feeling the dough than looking at it.*

Flavors of the Maghreb and Southern Italy

FRIED PIZZA DOUGH WITH CINNAMON SUGAR

Serves 6

Whether you make your own pizza dough, or simply purchase a ready-made one, this is a dessert that will bring out the child in you. I make this dessert often when I have leftover dough. I make it topped with cinnamon sugar or a drizzle of honey. Try them both!

1 ready-made pizza dough
½ cup granulated sugar
2 teaspoons ground cinnamon
Extra virgin olive oil for frying
Sea salt, honey, melted chocolate, or Nutella for topping

Allow the dough to rest at room temperature for 2 to 3 hours. Divide the dough into 6 equal parts. Shape each piece into a ball and place on a lightly floured surface. Flatten each ball into the size and shape of small pita bread.

In a small bowl, mix the sugar and cinnamon together.

Line a baking sheet with a double layer of paper towels.

You will have to fry the dough in batches of two at a time. Heat ¼-inch oil in a large frying pan over medium-high heat. When the oil is hot and shimmering, very carefully place two pieces of the dough in the pan. The oil will spatter, so stand back a bit. When the dough begins to bubble up and rise, about 1 minute, peek at the bottom of the dough. If the bottom of the dough is golden brown, it's time to flip it.

Cook the other side until golden brown, about 1 minute. When ready, transfer to the prepared baking sheet to drain. Quickly sprinkle the cinnamon sugar on both sides of the hot dough. Try sprinkling sea salt, or drizzling honey, melted chocolate, or Nutella on top.

Repeat with the remainder of the dough, adding a little more oil at a time, if necessary. Serve warm. Grab one, pull it apart, and share with a friend!

APRICOT CROSTATA
Serves 8 to 10

Acrostata can be filled with fruity marmalades and jams, ricotta, Nutella, or nuts. It's much easier than making fruit pies. *Crostata* is a traditional Italian dessert that can be served as is, with whipped cream, or with vanilla ice cream. Since apricot is my favorite marmalade, I always have it handy in my pantry.

2 cups unbleached all-purpose flour
½ cup confectioners' sugar
10 tablespoons cold unsalted butter, cut into cubes, plus more for the pan
2 large egg yolks
¼ cup ice water
2 cups apricot preserves

Place the flour, sugar, and butter in a food processor. Pulse a few times until the mixture resembles fine bread crumbs. Add the yolks and ice water; pulse until the mixture becomes a smooth dough.

Divide the dough in half and shape it into 2 discs. Wrap each disc in plastic wrap and allow to rest for 30 minutes in the refrigerator.

Heat the oven to 350°F. Butter a 10-inch springform pan.

Remove the dough from the refrigerator. Place one ball between two pieces of parchment paper. Roll out the ball to create a circle that will fit the springform pan and go about an inch up the sides. Transfer the dough to the pan, pressing it in to fit. Prick the dough all over with a fork. Spread the apricot preserves evenly on top of the dough.

Roll out the other dough ball between two sheets of parchment paper to about the same thickness as the first. Remove the parchment paper on top and cut the dough into strips.

Drape the strips over the crostata to form a lattice pattern, leaving gaps in between the strips so the preserves can show through. Trim any strips that are too long to fit the pan.

Bake until the pastry is golden, 35 to 40 minutes. Let cool until just warm or the preserves can burn you. Remove the pastry from the pan. Serve warm. Try it with vanilla gelato—not traditional, but oh so good!

PEARS STUFFED WITH RICOTTA AND HONEY

Serves 4 to 8

In southern Italy, ricotta is not just for stuffing pasta. It is often used in desserts, such as cannoli, tiramisu, and ricotta cheesecake. Pears with Ricotta and Honey is a sophisticated dessert that can be served with a French or Italian dinner or for an intimate Valentine's Day dinner for two.

Note: *This dish must be started the day before you are serving it, so you can drain the ricotta overnight. Draining the ricotta gets rid of excess liquid, so the ricotta is thicker and creamier. (See page 198.)*

   4 fresh Bosc pears, unpeeled
   8 teaspoons honey, plus more for drizzling
   8 ounces whole milk ricotta, drained overnight
   10 amaretti cookies, divided

Heat the oven to 350°F. Line a 9- x 13-inch baking pan with parchment paper.

Cut the pears in half lengthwise. Remove the stems and scoop out the seeds gently with a teaspoon. Cut off a very thin piece from the round side of each pear so it will sit flat. Drizzle 1 teaspoon honey on the cut-side of each pear. Transfer to the prepared baking pan, cut-side up. Bake until tender (test with a toothpick), about 30 minutes.

Place the ricotta in a bowl and whip with a wooden spoon until creamy, about 2 minutes. Crumble 8 amaretti cookies into the ricotta and mix well.

Mound the ricotta evenly onto the pear halves. Place them in the oven for 5 minutes to warm them. Remove them from the oven. Crumble the remaining 2 cookies and sprinkle over the pears. Drizzle honey on top. Serve cool or at room temperature.

PUCKERY LEMON CAKE
Serves 4 to 8

Puckery Lemon Cake is a simple, soft cake to enjoy with tea, espresso, cappuccino, or an after-dinner liqueur. While this cake is baking, I am always amazed at the intense lemon fragrance filling my kitchen.

FOR THE CAKE:
2 ½ cups unbleached all-purpose flour, plus more for the pan
½ cup fine semolina
2 teaspoons baking powder
½ teaspoon salt
1 cup whole milk
1 (6-ounce) container full-fat lemon yogurt
1 teaspoon pure vanilla extract
Zest of 2 lemons
Juice of 1 lemon
8 ounces unsalted butter, softened
1 ¾ cups granulated sugar
3 large eggs

FOR THE SYRUP:
1 cup granulated sugar
Juice of ½ lemon
1 bay leaf
⅓ cup Limoncello
1 to 2 lemons, each cut in 8 to 12 very thin slices

To make the cake: Heat the oven to 350°F. Butter and flour a 9- x 13-inch baking pan, shaking out excess flour.

In a medium bowl, combine the flour, semolina, baking powder, and salt.

In a small bowl, mix together the milk, yogurt, vanilla, lemon zest, and lemon juice.

In a large bowl, beat the butter and sugar at medium speed until light and fluffy, about 5 minutes. Beat in eggs, one at a time, beating well after each addition. Reduce the speed to low. Add the flour mixture alternately with the milk mixture, one-third at a time. Beat well after each addition. Transfer to the prepared pan.

Bake until a toothpick inserted in the center comes out clean, about 35 minutes. Cool completely. Poke holes in the cake with a skewer so that when the syrup is spooned on the cake, it will penetrate a little deeper.

To make the syrup: Place 1 cup water, the sugar, lemon juice, and bay leaf in a small saucepan. Bring to a boil and cook, stirring continually, until sugar has completely dissolved. Reduce heat to a simmer, and cook until the syrup becomes glossy, 10 to 15 minutes. Remove and discard the bay leaf. Add the Limoncello and lemon slices. Simmer for 5 minutes and remove from the stove. When the cake is ready, use a spoon to drizzle the warm syrup over the cake. Decorate with the lemon slices from the syrup. Serve as is, or with fresh berries.

RICOTTA AND ESPRESSO DESSERT

Serves 4 to 6

Just as delicious as a cannoli, but without the shell, this Sicilian recipe does not require any cooking. This is an impressive dessert that can be served for a Sunday dinner with the family, or for any occasion any time of the year.

Note: *This dish must be started the day before you are serving it, so you can drain the ricotta overnight. Draining the ricotta gets rid of any liquid, so the ricotta is thicker and creamier. (See page 198.)*

⅓ cup granulated sugar
2 ounces unsweetened cocoa powder
¼ cup freshly brewed espresso, cooled
2 teaspoons pure vanilla extract
1 pound whole milk ricotta, drained overnight
3 to 4 tablespoons toasted sliced almonds, crumbled amaretti,
    mini semisweet chocolate chips, or whipped cream to garnish

Mix the sugar and cocoa together in a bowl. Add the espresso and vanilla; use a wooden spoon to mix to combine. The mixture will be quite thick.

Place the drained ricotta in a large bowl. Add the espresso mixture a little at a time, mixing well, until the mixture is smooth and well incorporated. Taste; adjust the cocoa and sugar to your liking.

Once well mixed, transfer to small serving cups or glasses. Cover with plastic wrap and refrigerate for at least 4 hours. When ready to serve, top with some toasted almonds, crumbled amaretti, mini chocolate chips, or whipped cream.

CONDIMENTS

Harissa
Ras el Hanout Spice Blend

HARISSA
Makes ½ cup

Harissa is a spicy sauce made with red chili pepper, garlic, and spices typical of Morocco, Algeria, and Tunisia. Tunisian cuisine is known as the spiciest of the Maghrebi cuisines and harissa is prepared in every home. Harissa, which in Arabic means "pounded," has a bright red color, and serves to season numerous dishes such as couscous, tagines, grilled meats, vegetables, fish, and stews. Sometimes a small portion is added to the dish; most of the time, however, it is served on the side for guests to use as little or as much as they would like.

2 cloves garlic, crushed
½ teaspoon ground cayenne pepper
2 to 3 teaspoons red pepper flakes
1 tablespoon ground coriander
1 tablespoon ground cumin
⅛ teaspoon kosher salt
⅛ teaspoon freshly ground black pepper
2 tablespoons tomato paste
3 tablespoons extra virgin olive oil, plus more to cover top
2 to 3 tablespoons warm water

In a small food processor, place the garlic, cayenne, red pepper flakes, coriander, cumin, salt, and pepper. Pulse a few times until well blended. Add the tomato paste and pulse again a few times. Add the olive oil and pulse again. Add 1 tablespoon warm water and pulse again. Harissa should be the consistency of thick ketchup. If it is still too thick, continue to add warm water, a little at a time, until it is the right consistency.

Transfer the harissa to a glass jar, and top with additional olive oil to preserve. Refrigerate for up to 2 weeks.

RAS EL HANOUT
SPICE BLEND
Makes about ⅔ cup

"*R*as el Hanout" in Arabic means "the head of the grocery store," or "the merchant." It is a mixture of spices widely used in the cuisine of the Maghreb and is a flagship product of Arabic grocery stores. The blend of spices is unique to each merchant, and it can also be adapted to satisfy various cravings and budgets of the buyers. The mixture also varies among regions of the Maghreb and in the rest of the Mediterranean. Tradition dictates that each mix should contain a so-called aphrodisiac spice.

Ras el Hanout is a strongly aromatic, barely spicy, and slightly sweet mixture of many spices; it can contain more than fifty varieties. Because of its special, warm, aromatic, and sweet taste, it is used to flavor couscous, rice, tagines, pastilla, meats, seafood, and many vegetables dishes. Sometimes it is even used in pastries; it blends very well with honey and almonds.

Some of the most common spices used in creating a blend of Ras el Hanout are cinnamon, ginger, coriander, cardamom, nutmeg, black pepper, turmeric, dried rose petals, cloves, cumin, fennel seeds, paprika, allspice, and cayenne.

You can buy Ras el Hanout in a specialty grocery store but try making your own instead.

3 tablespoons ground coriander
2 tablespoons ground cumin
2 tablespoons freshly ground black pepper
1 tablespoon ground cardamom
1 teaspoon ground sweet paprika
1 teaspoon ground ginger
1 teaspoon ground cinnamon
½ teaspoon red pepper flakes
½ teaspoon ground nutmeg
½ teaspoon dried rose petals,
   ground (optional)

In a small bowl, combine all of the spices. Store in an airtight glass container in a cool area, not in the refrigerator, for up to 12 months.

PANTRY ESSENTIALS FOR MAGHREBI AND ITALIAN CUISINES

By stocking your kitchen with a few basic ingredients, you will be ready to prepare many of the recipes in this book. Keep fresh fruits, herbs, and vegetables on hand.

Bread crumbs

Broths and stocks

Bulgur wheat

Canned tomatoes

Cannellini beans

Capers

Chickpeas

Couscous

Dried fruits

Dry pasta

Extra virgin olive oil

Garlic and onions

Lemons

Lentils

Nuts

Rice

Roasted peppers

Rosewater

Potatoes

Spices

Tomato paste

Vinegars

Olives

FRESH HERBS GUIDE

Fresh herbs and spices can enrich simple foods into flavorful delicious dishes without adding additional calories or fat. These seasonings also increase the natural flavors of a dish. Should you need to use dried herbs, measure 1 teaspoon of dried for each 1 tablespoon of fresh.

HERB Basil

SUBSTITUTION Oregano or thyme

USES Use fresh and uncooked on pasta dishes, salads, sauces, crostini, pizza, tomatoes, peas, zucchini, and pesto.

HISTORY OR MYTH Basil was a symbol of love in Italy and other Mediterranean countries; a sprig presented to a lover meant fidelity. When a woman put a pot of basil on the balcony outside her room, it meant that she was ready to receive her suitor.

HERB Bay leaves

SUBSTITUTION Thyme

USES Use to aromatize and flavor sauces, vegetables, and soups.

HISTORY OR MYTH The bay leaf is a mythological sacred plant of Apollo; the branch of the laurel was used to encircle the heads of victors.

HERB Chives

SUBSTITUTION Scallions or leeks

USES Use fresh with potatoes, salads, and grilled vegetables.

HISTORY OR MYTH Chives date back more than 5,000 years. In Roman times, chives were considered a diuretic and an excellent natural preventative for sunburns and sore throats.

HERB Cilantro

SUBSTITUTION Parsley

USES Use in hummus, dips, salads, and soups.

HISTORY OR MYTH Cilantro has been used as a culinary herb since at least 5,000 B.C. Spanish conquistadors introduced it to Mexico and Peru.

HERB Dill weed

SUBSTITUTION Fennel tops

USES Use fresh and uncooked. Pairs well with sauces, breads, cucumber, cauliflower, salads, green beans, and soups.

HISTORY OR MYTH Dill was known as a medicinal herb to the ancient Greeks and Romans; soldiers placed burnt dill seeds on their wounds to promote healing. Medieval Europe could not grow it fast enough for love potions, casting spells, and protection against witchcraft.

HERB Mint

SUBSTITUTION Basil or parsley

USES Use fresh and uncooked. Use in fruit salads, with peas, tabbouleh, couscous, salads, lemonade, potatoes, and fruit, and as a tea.

HISTORY OR MYTH Mint was named for a very beautiful nymph, Minte, in Greek mythology. She was loved by the god of the underworld, Ade. For revenge, Ade's wife, Persephone, transformed Minte into a plant.

HERB Oregano

SUBSTITUTION Thyme or basil

USES Use with potatoes, peppers, tomatoes, olives, tomato sauces, soups, vegetables, salad dressings.

HISTORY OR MYTH Mediterranean oregano was originally grown extensively in Greece and Italy. Since Greek and Roman times, it has been used with meats, fish, vegetables, and as a flavoring for wine.

HERB Parsley, Italian

SUBSTITUTION Cilantro

USES Use fresh and uncooked. Great with boiled potato salad, tabbouleh, couscous, salad, stuffing, tomato sauces, soups, stews, vegetables.

HISTORY OR MYTH An Italian saying, "What to say about parsley but to say you are always in the middle, like parsley." Parsley was cultivated around the third century B.C. The Romans used parsley as a garnish and flavoring. They put it on their tables and around their necks in the belief the leaves would absorb fumes.

HERB Rosemary

SUBSTITUTION Thyme or tarragon

USES Use with roasted potatoes, vegetables, soups, stews, focaccia.

HISTORY OR MYTH It is said that during her journey from Egypt, the Virgin Mary draped her blue cloak on a rosemary bush. She then laid a white flower on top of the cloak. That night, the flower turned blue, and the bush was thereafter known as the "rose of Mary."

HERB Sage

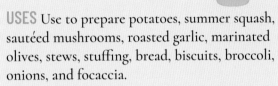

SUBSTITUTION Rosemary or thyme

USES Use with pasta, sautéed onions, stuffing, soups, tomatoes, potatoes, fries, chickpeas, and beans.

HISTORY OR MYTH The name "sage" comes from the Latin word "salia," meaning "to save." Greeks and Romans used sage to cure snake bites and to invigorate the mind and body. In the Middle Ages, people drank sage in tea and used sage to treat colds, fevers, liver disease, and epilepsy.

HERB Thyme

SUBSTITUTION Basil or oregano

USES Use to prepare potatoes, summer squash, sautéed mushrooms, roasted garlic, marinated olives, stews, stuffing, bread, biscuits, broccoli, onions, and focaccia.

HISTORY OR MYTH Ancient Greeks considered thyme a symbol of courage and sacrifice. Tradition tells that thyme was in the straw bed of the Virgin Mary and the Christ child. In the Middle Ages, ladies would embroider a sprig of thyme into scarves they gave to their errant knights. At various periods in history, thyme has been used to treat melancholy, reproductive system ailments, and to improve digestion. In the eighteenth century, thyme was recommended as a cure for a hangover.

SPICES GUIDE

SPICE **Cardamom**

SUBSTITUTION Ginger

USES Use in tea, coffee, rice, vegetables, couscous, sweets.

HISTORY OR MYTH Cardamom, which was used by the Romans and the Greeks, arrived in Europe along the caravan routes. At first, it was used mainly as an ingredient for perfumes. In "One Thousand and One Nights," it is cited as an aphrodisiac spice.

SPICE **Cinnamon**

SUBSTITUTION Nutmeg or allspice (use only ¼ of the amount)

USES Used in cakes, cookies, and desserts throughout the world. Cinnamon is also used in savory dishes in the Middle East. In American cooking, cinnamon is used with apples and other fruit and cereal dishes.

HISTORY OR MYTH Cinnamon has been popular since ancient times. Egyptians imported it from China in 2000 B.C. Romans believed cinnamon was sacred, and Nero burned a year's supply of the spice at his wife's funeral. Searching for cinnamon was a primary motive for world exploration in the fifteenth and sixteenth centuries.

SPICE **Coriander seed**

SUBSTITUTION Cumin

USES Used in Middle Eastern, Arabic, Mexican, South American, and Indian cuisine.

HISTORY OR MYTH Coriander is one of the oldest spices on record. Coriander was mentioned in the Bible, and the seeds have been found in ruins dating back to 5000 B.C.

SPICE **Cumin**

SUBSTITUTION Coriander

USES Used to perfume foods such as breads, vegetables, and couscous.

HISTORY OR MYTH In the Middle Ages, a time when spices were relatively rare, cumin was one of the most common. It was thought to promote love and fidelity. People carried it to weddings and walked around with it in their pockets. It was reputed to keep lovers and chickens from wandering. Thus, married soldiers were sent off to battle with a freshly baked loaf of cumin bread.

SPICE Ginger

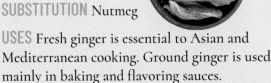

SUBSTITUTION Nutmeg

USES Fresh ginger is essential to Asian and Mediterranean cooking. Ground ginger is used mainly in baking and flavoring sauces.

HISTORY OR MYTH Ginger was one of the important spices that led to the opening of the spice trade routes. In the nineteenth century, it was popular to keep a shaker of ginger on the counter in English pubs so the patrons could shake some into their drinks. This practice was the origin of ginger ale.

SPICE Nutmeg

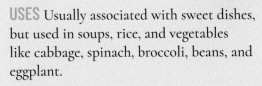

SUBSTITUTION Cinnamon or ginger

USES Usually associated with sweet dishes, but used in soups, rice, and vegetables like cabbage, spinach, broccoli, beans, and eggplant.

HISTORY OR MYTH Nutmeg has been touted as possessing or imparting magical powers. A sixteenth century monk is on record as advising young men to carry vials of nutmeg oil and, at the appropriate time, to anoint their genitals to ensure virility that would see them through several days.

SPICE Paprika

SUBSTITUTION Ground ancho chili pepper

USES Used as a garnish, sprinkled on hummus, hors d'oeuvres, and salad dressings. Many Spanish, Portuguese, and Turkish recipes use paprika in soups, stews, vegetables.

HISTORY OR MYTH Paprika is native to South America. Originally a tropical plant, it can now grow in cooler climates. Hungary and Spain are the two main centers for growing paprika peppers. Hungarian paprika is stronger and richer than Spanish paprika, which is very mild.

SPICE Pepper, black

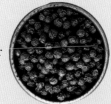

SUBSTITUTION White pepper or red pepper (use ¼ of the amount)

USES Used in any savory dish and in some sweet ones.

HISTORY OR MYTH In the Middle Ages, Europeans often used black pepper to pay rent, dowries, and taxes.

SPICE Saffron

SUBSTITUTION Turmeric (for color)

USES Used in Moorish, Maghrebi, Mediterranean, and Asian cuisines. Its most common function is to color and flavor Milanese risotto and Spanish paella.

HISTORY OR MYTH Ancient Greeks and Romans scattered saffron to perfume public baths. The thirteenth century Crusaders brought saffron from Asia to Europe, where it was used as a dye and condiment. In Asia, it was a symbol of hospitality. In India, people used saffron to mark themselves as members of a wealthy caste.

EXTRA VIRGIN OLIVE OIL (EVOO)

"The murmur of an olive grove has something very intimate, immensely old about it. It is too beautiful for me to dare paint it or be able to form an idea of it."—Vincent Van Gogh in a letter to his brother, Theo, in June 1889.

Olive oil is created from the fruit of the Mediterranean olive tree. There are historical documents, as well as religious and folkloristic, attesting to its existence and use since 1597 B.C. There were tablets found from that period in the Imperial Palace of Babylon that reported an inventory of rations of olive oil distributions. The Biblical passage about the flood and Noah's ark makes clear reference to the olive tree and olive oil. It was the Phoenicians who introduced the olive and its use along the coasts of the Mediterranean, Africa, and southern Europe. It was called "liquid gold." The Greeks expanded the use of olive oil. It was, however, the Romans who cultivated the olive trees in all the territories conquered by them. It was also the Romans who invented the first tools for the pressing of the olives. The lowest quality of oil was given to slaves throughout the Mediterranean and was used for commercial operations as well as for therapeutic purposes. The highest quality oil, which is made from green olives, was saved for the nobles and the rich. Olive oil became part of everyday life.

From about the fourteenth century until the late nineteenth century, olive oil went through a lengthy period of eclipse because the raising of cattle and pigs facilitated the making of other products such as butter and lard. It was not until the late nineteenth and early twentieth centuries that the birth and concept of regional cuisine was rediscovered and the use of olive oil in kitchens was revitalized. People sought to spread more and more of their ancient cultures to preserve them, to enhance them, and to give them the attention they deserved.

Extra virgin olive oil is like wine; it offers a wide assortment of flavors, colors, and aromas that vary with the soil, the climate, the location of cultivation, and the type of cultivar (olive tree or plant) grown. Olive oil is made when the olives are green or just barely beginning to turn color. The colors of oil can range from a delicate translucent pale yellow to deep emerald green. An extra virgin olive oil is free from additives and all of its nutritional components are preserved perfectly for months, if stored properly. It should be savored raw to enrich dishes such as pasta, soups, salads, and vegetables. To be labeled "extra virgin," olives must be freshly picked and extracted cold, with no chemical solvents or other techniques of extraction used to produce the oil. Under the International Olive Council standard, the highest grade of extra virgin olive oil contains no more than 1 percent of oleic acid. The lower the free fatty acid content, the higher the quality of the oil.

Flavors of the Maghreb and Southern Italy

HOW TO SELECT A GOOD EXTRA VIRGIN OLIVE OIL

Since every palate is different, there is only one true method for selecting a good extra virgin olive oil: the taste test. Taste the oil for liveliness, freshness, and lightness, making sure that it's not sticky, fatty, or flat tasting. When tasting a good extra virgin olive oil, you should feel a little scratchiness in the back of your throat; that's how you know it's fresh. Decide if you prefer a heavier, more robust olive oil, something a little smoother and lighter, a more peppery taste, sweeter, nuttier, fruitier, grassier, or one with a lighter flowery taste up front. Once you decide on the overall taste you want in an extra virgin olive oil, see what the experts suggest. Usually there is an interesting story to go with each extra virgin olive oil, like what country and region it came from, the types of olives used, and any recognition, praise, or awards.

WHEN TO COOK WITH EXTRA VIRGIN OLIVE OIL

Extra virgin olive oil is used in Maghrebi and other kitchens around the world. Although most of us tend to use extra virgin olive oil for cooking, there's no better way to appreciate it than when it is used raw. I use it raw drizzled over toasted bread (bruschetta), focaccia, or pizza. I use it raw as a condiment when I make salad dressings, pesto, hummus, an uncooked pasta sauce, or over grilled or roasted vegetables. When I use my extra virgin olive oil raw, I want it to be the star of the dish, an important component that contributes to the flavor of whatever I am making.

When cooking recipes such as pasta sauces, stews, and soups, I use extra virgin olive oil to enhance the flavors of my other ingredients. I do not deep fry with extra virgin olive oil. I use lighter oil such as light olive oil, because I don't want the oil to stand out; I want the other ingredients to stand out instead. For the process of frying, extra virgin olive oil does not add any value to my food; therefore, I don't use it in my deep-fried dishes.

ARE THERE ANY OLD-FASHIONED USES FOR EXTRA VIRGIN OLIVE OIL?

Sore throat? Swallow 1 tablespoon of extra virgin olive oil mixed with lemon juice in the morning on an empty stomach.

Chapped lips? Spread a few drops of extra virgin olive oil on your lips.

Wrinkles? Mix ½ tablespoon extra virgin olive oil with ½ tablespoon lemon juice. Massage face lightly with mixture at bedtime twice a week.

Dry skin? Mix extra virgin olive oil and cooking salt. Exfoliate with mixture and rinse with warm water.

Calloused skin? To soften, massage your body with extra virgin olive oil after your shower.

Tense? Relax in a bath with 3 tablespoons of extra virgin olive oil and a handful of rose petals.

CHEF ALBA'S HELPFUL TIPS
IN THE KITCHEN

How to drain ricotta

"Ricotta" means "recooked." Ricotta is made from the whey drained from other cheeses. It can be made with cow, sheep, goat, or water buffalo milk. The most common, found in our grocery stores, is cow's milk. Ricotta is used in many Italian sweet or savory recipes, and it can also be eaten uncooked. Often, recipes require the ricotta to be drained. There are two methods for draining. One, the method I prefer, is to place the ricotta in a sieve over a bowl, then cover it with plastic wrap and refrigerate it overnight. The other method is to place the ricotta in cheesecloth and squeeze the liquid out. Once the liquid, which is called "whey," has drained, the ricotta will be creamy. Discard the whey in the bowl, and use the ricotta as directed in the recipes.

How to store Italian parsley

My mom used this method for years and it works for me as well. Trim the tips of the stems of the parsley and stand the fresh parsley in a glass jar with fresh water. Cover with a plastic bag from the grocery store, not the resealable plastic bags; the store bags are lighter. Refrigerate. Change the water every few days. The parsley should last in the refrigerator for weeks.

Storing fresh tomatoes

Never put tomatoes in the refrigerator. Their sugars will become dormant in the cold climate, and they will become soft, less sweet, and mealy. Store tomatoes, stem-side down, at room temperature, in a basket or on a dish lined with a paper towel. The shoulders (part around the stem) are sturdier than the bottoms, so the bottoms won't get bruised. Eat tomatoes within a few days of purchasing before they soften too much. Should your tomatoes get a little mushy, blanch them, remove the skins, and use them to make a sauce, soup, or stew.

How to properly boil green vegetables

To minimize discoloration and ensure even cooking of green vegetables, cook them in a very large pot filled with boiling water, uncovered, stirring occasionally. Remember that the vegetables will be hot, and once removed and drained, they will continue to cook 1 to 2 more minutes. If you want to retain their color, douse them in an ice bath and drain again.

How to boil potatoes

Purchase potatoes that are about the same size. Rinse them well and remove any dirt and blemishes. I prefer cooking them with the skins on to ensure that nutrients are not lost during boiling. However, if you are in a time crunch and you need to make quick potato salad or mashed potatoes, you can peel them and cut them in smaller pieces to speed up the process.

Always place the potatoes in a large pot with cold water. Add enough water to cover the potatoes by one to two inches. If you put them in boiling water, the outside will cook faster than the inside. To check when the potatoes are done, pierce them with a wooden skewer or with the tip of a knife. Do not overcook them. Remember, if you are going to drain and bake them, the potatoes should be undercooked 2 to 3 minutes.

To prevent sogginess, drain the potatoes as soon as they are ready. If I am going to bake or stuff the potatoes, once they are drained, I spread them out on a baking sheet or large plate to cool and dry a bit. If you are mashing them, it is not necessary to dry them out.

How to cook garlic

Cooking garlic in hot oil is a recipe for disaster! Because the oil is hot, you cannot control how quickly the garlic will cook. Stirring it quickly won't help either. Most of the time the garlic ends up burnt or nearly burnt and must be thrown away because it will be bitter.

My technique: In a cold skillet, add the olive oil and garlic at the same time. Allow the garlic to aromatize the oil on low heat for a few minutes. When you smell the aroma of the garlic and it's barely golden, it's ready.

Cutting herbs into chiffonade

You can cut any herb with large leaves into chiffonade. Stack the leaves, roll them into a cigar shape, and cut them into thin slivers crosswise. Fluff the slivers up to separate them.

Doneness temperatures for food safety

https://www.foodsafety.gov/food-safety-charts/safe-minimum-cooking-temperature

Soaking dried beans

It is not necessary to soak dried beans overnight, however, they should be soaked in water in the refrigerator for 6 to 8 hours. If soaked too long, they could ferment and that may affect the flavor. The first thing I do is rinse the beans under cold running water a few times to remove any impurities or dust and then put them in a glass bowl with cold water to soak.

If you want to soak them overnight because it's easier, place the bowl in the refrigerator.

Advantages of soaking dried beans:
- reduces the cooking time
- eliminates some of the indigestible complex sugars that cause flatulence
- cleans the beans

After the beans have soaked, drain and rinse them again in cold water. Transfer the beans to a large pan with cold water three times the volume of the beans and begin the cooking process.

Using canned beans

If you are watching your sodium intake, rinse and drain all canned beans, including chickpeas, before using them.

BASIC COOKING METHODS

Baking: Baking uses dry heat, up to 375°F, to solidify batter and give it structure and color. This method is used mainly for cakes, cookies, muffins, pies, and breads.

Blanching: Blanching is immersing food in boiling cooking liquid, briefly cooking, removing it from the liquid and immediately transferring it to a bowl of ice water to stop the cooking. The cooking time ranges from 30 seconds to 2 minutes. This method is used for removing skins from tomatoes or other fruits. It is also used to soften vegetables and preserve their color.

Boiling and Simmering: Boiling is immersing food in a cooking liquid and bringing the liquid to a full bubbling boil, which happens at 212°F. This is the hottest temperature boiling water can reach. Simmering is when food is cooked in a liquid with a temperature in the range between 180°F and 205°F.

Braising: Braising is a two-step process. First the food is browned in a fat. The next step is to add enough liquid (broth, water, or wine) to the pan to cover the food. The food is then cooked in a moist environment over low heat, sometimes covered and sometimes only partially covered.

Grilling and Broiling: Grilling and broiling are two of the oldest cooking methods. Both methods use direct dry heat with a thin layer of air between the heat source and the food. This method essentially guarantees a crispy crust on the outside and a moist and tender interior.

Pan Searing: Searing is a cooking process in which a piece of food is placed on a hot pan over very high heat for a fairly brief amount of time until the food is browned and caramelized. Searing develops the aroma, color, and flavor on the surface of foods.

Poaching: Poaching is placing food in liquid with a temperature ranging from 140°F to 180°F. Poaching is done at a low temperature, avoiding distress to the food. There will be small bubbles forming at the bottom of the pan, but the bubbles do not rise to the surface. Poaching is ideal for cooking delicate or fragile ingredients, like fish and eggs.

Roasting: Roasting uses dry heat; the difference between roasting and grilling or broiling is that roasting is done in a closed environment—the oven—and the heat is indirect. Roasting is done at temperatures of 400°F or higher, although some roasting, especially of proteins, can be done at a lower temperature. The high heat crisps up the exterior of foods while cooking the interior slowly. Flavors added during the roasting process may be in the form of solids or liquids. The juices that remain in the roasting pan after cooking can be used to make a sauce or gravy.

Sautéing: "Sauté" means "to jump" in French. Sautéing is when the food is cut into pieces or thinly sliced and then cooked with some fat in a hot pan over high heat, while being stirred. Sautéing, like roasting, grilling, and broiling, can create a crust or caramelization on food.

ABOUT THE AUTHORS

Alba Carbonaro Johnson

Chef Alba has been a cooking instructor for over 15 years. She is a food blogger, recipe writer, food tester and editor, and private chef. Alba teaches regional Mediterranean and Maghrebi cooking for several venues via Zoom or in-person classes. Born in Italy and raised in Tunisia, Alba's passion is to share her muticultural cooking experience and the art of simplifying techniques with her clients. Her recipes are rustic and vibrant in taste. Alba wrote her first book, *La Cucina Semplice*, with family recipes she learned while growing up in Tunisia and Italy.

Alba is a cooking instructor who also conducts culinary tours to Umbria and Tuscany in Italy and to Giverny, France. She has appeared on FOX DC, CBS DC, and PBS Virginia performing live demos.

Alba has a bachelor's degree in international business management; certification from the Training in Excellence Program, Center of Creative Leadership; and certification from The Professional Personal Chef Training.

Alba is a member of Les Dames d'Escoffier International, International Association of Culinary Professionals, Slow Food, and Culinary Historians of Washington.

Paula Miller Jacobson

Paula Miller Jacobson is a partner with Sheilah Kaufman in Cookbook Construction Crew. She has been editing cookbooks, developing and testing recipes, proofreading, indexing, and teaching cooking for over eighteen years.

Paula studied English at the University of Maryland, followed by a concentration in linguistics. She received a BA in theoretical linguistics and continued with post-graduate work in a doctoral program.

Paula's love of words led her to editing. She edited novels, doctoral dissertations, and newsletters for schools and charitable organizations. She tutored middle school, high school, and college students in grammar and composition for fifteen years.

At the same time, Paula was cooking: cooking at home, cooking for friends, taking cooking classes, developing recipes, catering for events both small and large, and testing recipes for a cookbook publisher. She's been cooking and catering for forty years.

When Paula met Sheilah Kaufman, she discovered that she could marry her two passions in a new profession. She tested recipes and edited cookbooks for Sheilah; they then formed Cookbook Construction Crew through which they mentor authors, editing their books, testing their recipes, and doing proofreading and indexing..

Paula has edited cookbooks and tested recipes for nutrition counselors, wellness coaches, and vegan, Italian, Greek, Turkish, Iraqi, kosher, Sephardic, Azerbaijani, Maghrebi, and pastry chefs, as well as for books about bread, canola oil, general cooking, and diabetes management. Paula collaborated on a book, *Healthy Bones: Build Them for Life—The Food-for-Bones Cookbook for the National Osteoporosis Foundation.*

Paula is a member of Les Dames d'Escoffier International, International Association of Culinary Professionals, Slow Food, and Culinary Historians of Washington.

Sheilah Kaufman

Sheilah Kaufman, the author of twenty-six cookbooks, has been a food editor and writer, culinary lecturer, and culinary instructor for more than forty-five years. With her many helpful hints and tips, Sheilah removes the intimidation from cooking and entertaining in *Sheilah's Fearless Fussless Cookbook*, (Delacorte, 1982), *Upper Crusts*, and the new edition of *Simply Irresistible: Easy, Elegant, Fearless, Fussless Cooking*. In her books, the award-winning *The Turkish Cookbook: Regional Recipes and Stories* (Interlink Books), *A Taste of Turkish Cuisine*, and *Sephardic Israeli Cuisine* (Hippocrene Books), Sheilah shares with her readers the deeply beautiful tapestry of Turkish and Israeli food and culture.

Sheilah trained at L'Academie de Cuisine in Bethesda, Maryland. She has traveled around the United States teaching cooking of a wide range of cuisines: Turkish, French, Mexican, and Mediterranean. Sheilah lectures about Mediterranean cooking and history, Jewish culinary traditions, and the history of the Jews and chocolate. She has been an invited guest speaker at Epcot's Food and Wine Festival and The Library of Congress and a selected speaker at the National Book Festival in Washington, D.C. Sheilah has lectured at the Textile Museum, Smithsonian Institution, Montgomery College, the Jewish Museum of Montreal, Les Dames d'Escoffier symposiums, Turkish Embassy, The Turkish Society of Canada, Culinary Historians, diplomatic groups, Hadassah, Jewish Federation of Greater Washington, Brandeis, Jewish Genealogy International, and special interest groups and organizations, as well as senior residential centers. She does cooking demonstrations on television programs. The National Press Club hosted a Turkish dinner based on *The Turkish Cookbook: Regional Recipes and Stories.*

Sheilah is a freelance writer and was the food editor for *Popular Anthropology* and the Maryland newspaper *The Town Courier*. For years she was food editor of the *Washington Jewish Week* and *Jewish Food Experience*. She has written for numerous magazines and papers and is a contributing editor to a number of publications including *Vegetarian Times*, *The Washington Post*, *Eating Well*, *Repast*, and *Culinary Historians of Washington*.

Sheilah and Paula Jacobson are partners in Cookbook Construction Crew.

A founding member of the International Association of Culinary Professionals, Sheilah also is an active member of Les Dames d'Escoffier, Culinary Historians of Washington, Slow Foods, and several diplomatic groups.

ACKNOWLEDGEMENTS AND DEDICATIONS

Alba Carbonaro Johnson

I dedicate this book to my dear husband, Bob; my children, Claudia and Christopher; my daughter-in-law, Alex; and many friends and customers for their ongoing support of my work. I especially want to dedicate this book as Nonna Alba, not Chef Alba, to my sweet baby granddaughter, Kira, whom I love dearly and unconditionally. Kira, I want to inspire you to cook Nonna's recipes when you grow up to be a fine young lady.

Paula Miller Jacobson

Thank you to my husband, Greg; my sons, Adam and Daniel; my daughters-in-law, Jennifer and Andrea; and my grandchildren, Ryan, Maya, and Allison. You are always ready to listen, chat, hug, cook and bake with me, and are the most eager and reliable tasters.

Sheilah Kaufman

My heartfelt thanks to my family, Debra, Kaleb, John, Jeffrey, Penelope, and Marjorie; my co-authors; and my friends for the wonderful support they provided.

Photographers:
Alba Carbonaro Johnson, Sandy Ireland
Food styling:
Alba Carbonaro Johnson

Recipe testers:
Paula Miller Jacobson, Alba Carbonaro Johnson, Sheilah Kaufman, and Marian Steinhorn

INDEX

Index

Index